MARCHING ORDERS FOR
THE END BATTLE

MARCHING ORDERS
FOR THE
END BATTLE

BY

Corrie ten Boom

CHRISTIAN LITERATURE CRUSADE
Fort Washington, Pennsylvania 19034

CHRISTIAN LITERATURE CRUSADE
Fort Washington, Pennsylvania 19034

CANADA
1440 Mackay Street, Montreal, Quebec

GREAT BRITAIN
The Dean, Alresford, Hampshire

AUSTRALIA
P.O. Box 91, Pennant Hills, N.S.W. 2120

Scripture quotations from the King James Version of the Bible, except as otherwise indicated. Those from *The New Testament in Modern English* by J. B. Phillips, © J. B. Phillips 1958, are reprinted with permission of The Macmillan Company.

CONTENTS

at his own risk to remove his regiment at his own risk to...

PREFACE

IN VIETNAM I MET A MAN from the jungle: Tsau. He came to me after I had spoken five times to his Chil tribe. He said, "Double old grandmother." Just imagine being called such a thing when you are only seventy-five years old, but to be old is the greatest honour in the Chil tribe; he wanted to say something really flattering. "You came from far, far away to tell us about Jesus. You travelled long, very long; you are old, very old. Will you thank your tribe in the name of our Chil tribe that they allowed you to come to us? We will establish a covenant, a covenant of prayer. You pray for us, we pray for you."

"Tsau, have you a special message for our tribe?" He waited a moment; I believe he prayed. "Yes, tell the people of your tribe that they have to turn away from their sins and repent, so that they may see Jesus when He comes again."

Was Tsau right? Sure, we have to repent and be converted, but also we must prepare for Jesus' coming again.

We believe that in our day we can see clearly the outlines of Biblical prophecies in world history. It is good to compare the newspapers with the Bible at this time. Then we understand that Jesus may come very soon. Before His return there will be a hard battle, and therefore it is good to prepare ourselves and to gird our loins

7

with power. Every Christian is called to take his place in the army of King Jesus and to wrestle as a fellow-conqueror with Him. "For we wrestle not against flesh and blood, but against principalities, against powers . . . against spiritual wickedness in high places" (Eph. 6:12).

This battle is more violent than ever before. The devil knows that his time is short. Everything is heading towards the great and final battle which John describes in the Book of Revelation, and that battle has started already. But we know:

> Jesus was Victor
> Jesus is Victor
> Jesus will be Victor.

CORRIE TEN BOOM.

1

MARCHING ORDERS

1. STIMULATION TO MILITANCY

"Your life is hid with Christ in God" (Col. 3:3).

GOD'S PLANS FOR THE VICTORY are perfect. He knows the enemy and the reactions of the enemy before the foundation of the world and He does not need to fear any unexpected attack. He also knows His men. He knows their need for food and clothing. He provides the equipment and He launches them at the right time and the right place, for He leads them to victory. Those who fight on our side are greater and stronger than those who stand against us: we have a mighty High Priest and legions of angels. Jesus came to destroy the works of the devil. At the Cross of Calvary He has already won the victory. There He crushed the head of the serpent. Above all things we need to know our position in this battle. The Bible speaks of this position: to be hid with Christ in God. What a comfort to know that we belong to the victorious army of God, when we look at the seemingly superior forces of the enemy. Nowadays there are many atheistic ideologies. The enemy also uses Marxism in the form of communism to persuade mankind that God does not exist. There are many people who are fervent communists.

Once I read a testimony of a communist. He wrote:

"We are fanatics. Our lives are absorbed by one tremendous all-important factor: the battle for world-communism. We communists would not spend any money on concerts or other pleasures. We have set a clear aim before our eyes. We have an ideal to fight for. We dedicate ourselves and our personal lives and possessions in the service of a great movement. What does it matter that our personal lives, our own egos have to suffer for the sake of the party? We are fully rewarded at the thought that every one of us is co-operating a little in the creation of something new, something better for mankind. There is only one thing for which I will die: communism. That is my life. That is my faith, my hobby, my love, my beloved; that is my master, my food and my drink.

"During the day I work for it and during the night I dream about it. As time goes on, its influence on me gets stronger and stronger. That's why I cannot make friends, why I cannot love, or even hold a conversation without touching on all this, and this force that stimulates and leads me. I have been in prison for the sake of my ideas, my ideals, and I am willing, if need be, to stand in front of the firing squad."

I know for myself, that it is not just one or a few who think and feel like that. There are hundreds of thousands who have perhaps never said it, but who live in the same manner. We must realise this very clearly. When you take the map of the world, you can see how many countries are under the control of communism and the influence of atheism which is connected with it. When I look at world history in the light of God's Word, then I do not believe that we can expect better times. Politics have no answer for this progress of atheism. Someone has said: "We have reached in our history of civilisation the point where the most serious crisis starts that mankind has ever experienced."

That is true; there is a great battle going on in the invisible world. It is easy to believe what Peter writes; it seems to be an even greater reality now than in those days: "Be sober, be vigilant; because your adversary the devil, as a roaring lion, walketh about, seeking whom he may devour: whom resist stedfast in the faith, knowing that the same afflictions are accomplished in your brethren that are in the world" (1 Pet. 5:8,9).

Every Christian is involved in this battle, whether he wants it or not. The enemy will try with all his might to alienate us from God, to destroy our faith in Jesus Christ and to make us rebellious against God. We can shut our eyes to the danger and not see where the course of world history will lead us. But Jesus says in Luke 21:36: "Watch ye therefore, and pray always, that ye may be accounted worthy to escape all these things that shall come to pass, and to stand before the Son of man."

In this time there are two sorts of people who are important: the fully dedicated children of God and the fully dedicated atheists. Every Christian is called to be involved in this fight. You can decide for yourself if you will be a good, a mediocre or a bad wrestler. Jesus Himself transforms everyone who surrenders fully to Him into a warrior led by the Holy Spirit, a warrior who looks forward to the final victory when Jesus comes again. Such a person has a strong case against the enemy and is never ashamed of his King. This is the work of the Holy Spirit. He gives us a vision of the final victory of Jesus Christ. "That is why God has now lifted him so high, and has given him the name beyond all names, so that at the name of Jesus 'every knee shall bow', whether in heaven or earth or under the earth. And that is why, in the end, 'every tongue shall confess' that

Jesus Christ is the Lord, to the glory of God the Father"
(Phil. 2:9–11, Phillips).

The Holy Spirit will prepare us: "He which hath begun a good work in you will perform it until the day of
Jesus Christ" (Phil. 1:6).

2. BE PREPARED

"That God, the God of our Lord Jesus Christ and
the all-glorious Father, will give you spiritual wisdom
and the insight to know more of him: that you may
receive that inner illumination of the spirit which will
make you realise how great is the hope to which he is
calling you—the magnificence and splendour of the in-
heritance promised to Christians—and how tremendous is the power available to us who believe in God"
(Eph. 1:17–19, Phillips).

Atheism is expanding. The kingdom of God is going
on quietly. Now it is either—or; Christ or Antichrist.
Nobody can serve two masters; either the one or the
other. The divisions are becoming clear-cut. We have
this great comfort, that God has shown us that He has a
plan for this world. He has no problems, only plans.
That is why there is never a panic in heaven. Knowing
the future gives us strength and security.

"For God has allowed us to know the secret of his
plan, and it is this: he purposes in his sovereign will
that all human history shall be consummated in
Christ, that everything that exists in heaven or earth
shall find its perfection and fulfilment in him. And
here is the staggering thing—that in all which will one
day belong to him we have been promised a share
since we were long ago destined for this by the one

who achieves his purposes by his sovereign will"
(Eph. 1:9—11, Phillips).

An abundant richness of strength is at our disposal.
We need this strength. Let us then be conscious of it in
our way of living. This richness does not depend on circumstances. We must realise this fully, because circumstances will be difficult in the final battle. But we shall
never lack anything.

Bishop Dzao of China sounded a warning to us when
he spoke in the Congress of Evangelists in Berlin. He
said: "China now experiences what probably will come
over the whole world. Yes, there will come a time when
nobody can buy or sell without the mark of the Antichrist" (Rev. 13:17).

The Bishop has confessed that the church in China
had not prepared the Christians for the terrible trials
they have to face now. "We gave them everything we
could—the gospel, churches, yes, food and clothing
where poverty reigned. But one thing we did not do. We
neglected to teach them how to pass on the gospel to
other people. Now all the preachers and bishops have
gone—the church practically does not exist any more.
Yes, an invisible church is going on, but how few Christians were strong enough to strengthen others!" This
bishop appealed to us to do our utmost to prepare the
children of God in this time and to show them the special task for this time, so that they will be strong enough
in the time of oppression. Is it possible that weak little
people can be ready for that? Yes, everyone can be
ready. I mean what I say. The Lord has given us all we
need for the end-time.

"But ye shall receive power, after that the Holy Ghost
is come upon you: and ye shall be witnesses unto me
both in Jerusalem, and in all Judea, and in Samaria,
and unto the uttermost part of the earth" (Acts 1:8).

This was a promise for the time when the Church of Jesus Christ came into existence, but these words have never lost their power, and especially in the final battle this promise will be a source of strength for the children of God so that they can lead a victorious life. This power is available, because the Holy Spirit has come and He longs to fill our hearts as the light flows into a room when it is opened to let the daylight in. Be filled with the Holy Spirit! Give room to the Holy Spirit! That means: Surrender!

3. HOPE FOR SINNERS

"Ye are the light of the world" (Matt. 5:14).

I spoke on this text in a prison. Perhaps you think it is a strange text for murderers and thieves, but I have seen that God can use "good" and "bad" people. I know many evangelists who are still serving their time in prison. The Holy Spirit has convicted them of sin, of righteousness and of judgment; and in His love for sinners the Lord Jesus has saved them, and made them children of God. I know many who have become real soul-winners, who have led many of their fellow-prisoners to the Lord. When I had finished my address, one of the prisoners got up and said: "Friends, today I read in the Bible about three murderers; one was Moses, one was David, one was Paul. We know them all as heroes of faith, but still they have been murderers. What God can do with a murderer who surrenders fully to Him! Fellows, there is also hope for us."

Yes, there is hope for every decent and indecent sinner, when he surrenders to Jesus, when he confesses his sins, when he gets converted by His strength, when he is cleansed by the blood of Jesus and filled with the Holy Spirit. Then he will become the light of the world.

There is no sin too great to bring to Jesus. He said: "Come unto me, all." And those who come to Jesus, He will never cast out. The very beginning is this: to come to Jesus and in His strength to turn away from sin, and then one is cleansed and sanctified. And thus, by the power of the Holy Spirit, one becomes through Jesus Christ more than conqueror. Then all fear for the future goes. Then we know that what Paul says in Romans 8:31–39 is true. I have experienced it:

"If God is for us, who can be against us? He who did not grudge his own Son, but gave him up for us all—can we not trust such a God to give us, with him, everything else that we can need? Who dares accuse us now? The judge himself has declared us free from sin. Who is in a position to condemn? Only Christ, and Christ died for us, Christ rose for us, Christ reigns in power for us, Christ prays for us! Can anything separate us from the love of Christ? Can trouble, pain or persecution? Can lack of clothes and food, danger to life and limb, the threat of force of arms? Indeed some of us know the truth of that ancient text:

For thy sake we are killed all the day long;
We were accounted as sheep for the slaughter.

No, in all these things we win an overwhelming victory through him who has proved his love for us. I have become absolutely convinced that neither death nor life, neither messenger of heaven nor monarch of earth, neither what happens today nor what may happen tomorrow, neither a power from on high nor a power from below, nor anything else in God's whole world has any power to separate us from the love of God in Jesus Christ our Lord!" (Phillips). Hallelujah!

4. TRAINING

"He that shall endure unto the end, the same shall be saved" (Matt. 24:13).

A soldier must obey. He cannot serve the king and the nation if he does his own will. Jesus was obedient. He, the Creator of the world, always submitted to His Father's will. He set His face towards Jerusalem to be crucified. He was obedient unto the death of the Cross. That was His way to the resurrection. This is also the way for His followers, for only the way of obedience, the way of crucifixion, leads to the resurrection. Cross-bearing in the form of martyrdom has become unknown in Western Europe; in Eastern Europe it is not. Nevertheless it is of great importance nowadays, for the opposition against God and the Cross is increasing. What can we expect, when atheism will find its climax in the coming and the revelation of the Antichrist?

"That day will not come before there arises a definite rejection of God and the appearance of the lawless man. He is the product of all that leads to death, and he sets himself up in opposition to every religion" (2 Thess. 2:3,4, Phillips).

Will God be defeated? No. After this period of darkness, His trumpet will sound and His Son Jesus Christ will come. Then it will be very clearly manifested that the Gospel is brought indeed to all nations. "Go ye therefore, and make disciples of all the nations" is the command.

Once a woman read her Bible in the morning hour from 1 Thess. 4:16–18 (Phillips):

"One word of command, one shout from the arch-angel, one blast from the trumpet of God and God in person will come down from heaven! Those who have died in Christ will be the first to arise, and we who are still living on the earth will be swept up with them into the clouds to meet the Lord in the air. And after that we shall be with Him for ever. God has given me this message on the matter, so by all means use it to encourage one another."

When she read this, her thoughts were fixed particularly on the seriousness of this passage. The signs of the times are clear and everyone knows that great events are coming. Not only Bible readers know this, but also the people who read the newspapers. She was so completely taken up in meditating about Jesus' coming, that she did not hear the doorbell ring. After some time she suddenly heard it and opened the door quickly, her Bible still in her hand.

"It seems as if you are becoming deaf, lady! I had to ring the bell three times!" the milkman said. "Oh, I am so sorry. No, I am not deaf, but I was reading something in the Bible that was so great, that I forgot everything around me. Do you know, it is possible that one day you will come to my door and I will not be here? And everywhere you ring the bell where Christians used to live, you will find the house empty. I just read that when Jesus comes again, we will meet Him in the air. Then we shall be suddenly changed and we shall see Him face to face. You would not understand why so many people had suddenly disappeared. Later on you would hear what had happened and then you would ask why that old lady had not told me that before. And that's why I tell you now. Listen, milkman, when you accept Jesus as your Saviour, then you will become a child of God too, and will belong to those who will meet Him in the air."

Whether we agree with the point of view of this old lady or not, we notice that she really meant what she said, and that she looked forward to the coming again of Jesus. It is not at all important whether we have much money at this time. But it is very important that at that moment other people will go with us to meet the Lord, people to whom we showed the way of salvation.

The armour of God in Ephesians 6 is not solely described as the armour of the soldiers of Jesus Christ in the victorious final battle, but also for the time of Paul as well as for this time. Because we know that the great final battle will start soon, this armour and absolute obedience to the marching orders in these last days are very important. Jesus said in Luke 21:8 that these days would come, and we can see already from the newspapers that they are upon us. Let us not be afraid, these things must happen first.

It is so kind of the Lord to tell us this beforehand. We are, strictly speaking, the only people in the whole world who know the future and who understand the present time. This knowledge does not need to make us downhearted, because the Lord has spoken many comforting words in view of the future: "So likewise ye, when ye see these things come to pass, know ye that the kingdom of God is nigh at hand. And when these things begin to come to pass, then look up, and lift up your heads; for your redemption draweth nigh. But there shall not a hair of your head perish. Hold on, and you will win your souls!" (Luke 21:31,28,18,19).

It is important to persevere in this time; then we can go through life with uplifted head, our eyes fixed on Jesus. The moment comes that we shall see the Son of man coming on a cloud with great power and glory. All these perspectives we know through God's Word. "I will hasten my word to perform it" (Jer. 1:12). "Heaven and earth shall pass away, but my words shall not pass away" (Matt.24:35). "Watch ye therefore, and pray always, that ye may be accounted worthy to escape all these things that shall come to pass ..." (Luke 21:36). "Be on your guard—see to it that your minds are never clouded by dissipation or drunkenness or the worries of this life, or else that day may catch you like the springing of a trap" (Luke 21:34, Phillips).

Worries of this life, we all know them! Is that, then, wrong? No, but they can occupy us, that that day would come upon us as a terrible surprise, because we forgot to be vigilant and had not prepared ourselves for it. So it was also in the time of the deluge:

> "For just as life went on in the days of Noah so will it be at the coming of the Son of man. In those days before the flood people were eating, drinking, marrying and being given in marriage until the very day that Noah went into the ark, and knew nothing about the flood until it came and destroyed them all. So will it be at the coming of the Son of man" (Matt. 24:37–39, Phillips).

Everywhere in the world there are children of God who have difficulties, especially those who really mean business with the Word of God and with their call to be the light of the world and the salt of the earth. Very often their fellow-Christians make it hard for them because they do not agree with some Biblical truths and because they cannot accept the total surrender with all its consequences. In these difficulties, one must practise patience and love. The devil likes it when we, like iconoclasts, ruthlessly throw away old truths and traditions. "If I have the gift of foretelling the future and hold in my mind not only all human knowledge but the very secrets of God, and if I also have that absolute faith which can move mountains, but have no love, I amount to nothing at all" (1 Cor. 13:2, Phillips).

When the devil cannot keep us back, he tries to push us so fast that we exaggerate. Then we are in danger of forgetting to love. It is very important for us to understand that all these temptations and trials belong to training for the final battle. The "trainer", the Holy Spirit, gives us what we need. He teaches us to be patient, to look at the Lord, to pay attention to our fellow-warriors, and not to burden ourselves with superfluous luggage. This all is a part of the victorious life, while He trains conquerors; He comforts us with His bountiful promises.

2

CONQUERORS

BEFORE WE GO ON FINDING OUT what is expected from us
in the final battle, we can encourage each other with
some promises which God gives to the overcomers:

"To the victorious I will give the right to eat from
the tree of life which grows in the paradise of God ...
I will give the victorious some of the hidden manna,
and I will also give him a white stone with a new
name written upon it which no man knows except the
man who receives it ... To the one who is victorious,
who carries out my work to the end, I will give authority over the nations" (Rev. 2:7,17,26, Phillips).

"The victorious shall wear such white garments,
and never will I erase his name from the book of life.
Indeed, I will speak his name openly in the presence
of my Father and of his angels. As for the victorious, I
will make him a pillar in the Temple of my God, and
he will never leave it. I will write upon him the name
of my God, and the name of the city of my God, the
new Jerusalem which comes down out of heaven from
my God. And I will write upon him my own new
name. As for the victorious, I will give him the
honour of sitting beside me on my throne, just as I
myself have won the victory and have taken my seat
beside my Father on his throne" (Rev. 3:5,12,21,
Phillips).

5. VICTORY OVER SINS IN DAILY LIFE

"Your sins have hid his face from you" (Isa. 59:2).

We must have clear vision, but our sins often hinder us. They confuse our sight. Therefore it is so important that we are obedient to the command of the Lord: "Everyone who has at heart a hope like that keeps himself pure, for he knows how pure Christ is" (1 John 3:3, Phillips).

He who waits for Jesus' coming again gets sensitive to every shadow that comes between his Master and himself, and he does not rest until the vision is clear again. We must understand clearly that this text does not mean a striving to make ourselves better and better. We must look at Jesus, our hope. He is the Lord, who sanctifies us. The Holy Spirit gives us what we need.

"The Spirit ... produces in human life fruits such as these: love, joy, peace, patience, kindness, generosity, fidelity, tolerance and self-control" (Gal. 5:22, Phillips).

The devil accuses us night and day. He likes to push us into dismay, because then we cannot be strong. But the Word of God says to us: "Be strong in the Lord." He can give us this command, because He Himself gives us His strength. As soon as we realise that there is a sin in our hearts, we must bring it to the Lord, because that sin makes us insecure and weak. When we confess our sins, He is faithful and just to forgive us our sins. We must know that it is really true that the blood of Jesus cleanses us from all sins we bring to Him (1 John 1:7, 9). When we confess our sins to the Lord and ask for forgiveness, He will cast them into the depths of the sea. "He will turn again, he will have compassion upon us; he will subdue our iniquities; and thou wilt cast all their sins into the depths of the sea" (Mic. 7:19).

He will forgive and forget, and I believe that He sometimes must put a little sign: "No fishing allowed!" This is necessary, because sin confessed to the Lord is gone. At the Cross Jesus finished everything. "For our fight is not against any physical enemy: it is against organisations and powers that are spiritual" (Eph. 6:12, Phillips). "Your enemy the devil is always about, prowling like a lion roaring for its prey" (1 Pet. 5:8, Phillips).

When we think of the future, when the great final battle takes place, we can very well imagine roaring lions and evil spirits, but we must not forget that these are now already mobilised in the battle and it is part of our training that we recognise them and become firm. The devil is like a lion, but he is chained up. When we do not come too close, we are not in danger. I remember a friend who had to fight against a bad temper. Having tempers is in the eyes of many people a decent sin, but in reality it is a horrible sin, which gives the people around us very much sorrow and suffering. That friend longed with all his heart for victory over that sin. Then someone gave him this advice: "You must take care that you do not come too close to the lion! Don't forget that he is chained up!" Jesus tied him to a chain: He came to conquer the devil and to break the works of the devil. Yes, the children of God are attacked much at this very time and it is good to know our enemy; that is why it is necessary to be victor now in daily life and to surrender completely to the Lord Jesus. Jesus is always Conqueror! All we have to do is to see to it that we remain in good contact with Him and then His life of victory will flow through us and touch the people around us. Our everyday life is our battle place. A part of God's strategy is to appoint the place where we have to fight. We cannot escape the war by looking for another front line. "Our

place with Him is here, under His banner of the Cross!"
Jonah was disobedient and wanted to run away from his
call, but one can never hide himself from God (Jonah
1:3).

Are you sure that you are in the place where you are
called? In the office, at the engine, at the side of your
husband or wife? Jesus gives you your place. "Abide in
me," He says, "and I in you. As the branch cannot bear
fruit of itself, except it abide in the vine; no more can
ye, except ye abide in me" (John 15:4). Your place is in
Him. There is no room and no time for our own plans
to do private battle with the evil one, for a game with
the chained-up lion, for coquetting with great or small
sins of everyday life. With Jesus hid in God! Can we
find a safer hiding-place? The devil will have to go first
through God and Jesus, before he reaches us! When soldiers are trained, they receive their training in barracks
together with others. The training in the victorious
army of God for the last great battle does not take place
under unusual circumstances, but in the midst of the
common daily life. Here is the place of training—and everything we experience belongs to that training. So do
our contacts with our fellow-men. In the first letter of
Peter we read that all difficulties and temptations work
together to get us prepared:

"This means tremendous joy to you, I know, even
though at present you are temporarily harassed by all
kinds of trials and temptations. This is no accident—it
happens to prove your faith, which is infinitely more
valuable than gold, and gold, as you know, even
though it is ultimately perishable, must be purified by
fire. This proving of your faith is planned to result in
praise and honour and glory in the day when Jesus
Christ reveals himself" (1 Pet. 1:6,7, Phillips).

You are encouraged when you see the temptations of everyday life in that light. It can be difficult, but when you see it from God's point of view, then you know that the geatest power of God's love and joy, the fruit of the Holy Spirit, is at our disposal in daily life. What a mystery! When things are seen from the view-point of eternity, it makes you patient, for you know: "I am like gold that must be purified." Then you will fix your eyes upwards—and you do this again and again.

6. VICTORY THROUGH DECREASING

"He must grow greater and I less and less" (John 3:30, Phillips).

Do you ever have days when everything goes wrong? You try to do your utmost, but you do not succeed at all. I remember one week in which every day was more mixed up than the day before. First everything seemed to go so well. I was to work eight days in a town in Australia. A minister there had invited me as his guest in his home. Although he had many children, he could make room for me. When you travel a great deal, it is always difficult if you have nowhere to unpack your suitcase. It was a very dark small room in which I would have to live that week. I could not hang up my clothes, I had no table to write at; but you get used to these difficulties. When things are very bad I always say: "Lord Jesus, You have had times when You had nowhere to lay Your head. I am in Your service. This is just a little bit of cross-bearing."

But the little room was not the worst problem. The minister was difficult to work with. When we talked about the plans for the week, I was not allowed to make any decision by myself. He just dictated everything I had to do; and I did try to be obedient. When he told me that he had to preach the Gospel in a mental hospital, I became quite enthusiastic. "Can I go with you and work there too?" "Oh," he said, and looked at me very unkindly, "you, a woman? Well, all right; why not? If you would like to do that, we can organise something." But after the first meeting in his church, I felt that we did not form a team at all. His ideas were so different from mine, it was difficult to cooperate with him.

After three days, I became frightened to go with this man, with whom I was not united in spirit at all, to a place where so often there are many powers of darkness. I decided to speak to him about this. I went to his study and said: "Pastor, I believe that I cannot go to that institution. We ought to be closely united as a team and we are not." He became angry. "You have said that you wanted to go, and now you must go!" I refused. "You must; you have to do what I tell you."

I got up and went to the garden. I had a real, inward struggle. I was offended. I was afraid. What right had this man to dictate what I had to do? But then I understood; I had to decrease still more. Someone who has lost his life for Jesus' sake cannot be offended! I prayed: "Lord, You know that I cannot do this, but I will go the lowest way. Must I do what this man says and go with him to the institution? I am afraid of it, Lord! But I will go the way of obedience." It took a full hour before peace came into my heart. Then I went back to the study. "Pastor, if you say that I have to go, then I will do it." His answer settled the matter. "Oh no; it is not necessary to go. I phoned the director of the institution and told him that you would not come." "Oh, Pastor, how glad I am!" "Yes, it was not difficult at all. I simply said to him: 'This Corrie ten Boom has been in a concentration camp for a time. Now she is not quite normal; we must just accept that!' "

I turned away and went to my little room. Yes, it was

a relief that I did not have to go to that mental hospital, but how offended I was! And so I had to be on the platform with this man for another four days. People came to visit me, but they were not allowed to do so. I almost lost courage, and I was afraid that it would become a lost week.

There was always a young Baptist minister with members of his congregation in the meetings. He always listened with an open heart. It is a joy to have someone in a meeting who by the expression on his face gives you a "real answer". That gave me a bit more confidence. The last evening was perhaps the most difficult of all. I spoke about full surrender, about walking in the light, as Jesus is in the light, so that we can have fellowship one with the other—but I felt that I had no fellowship with my host, and also that I did not walk in the light with him. The Baptist pastor said to me: "I can take you to your next place tonight by car. It is about three hundred miles away from here, but I am used to driving by night. When I was a student I worked for my brother as a driver on his truck, and always had to drive during the night. While I am taking you there, we can be talking. Will you be sure that your luggage is ready?"

That was a lovely suggestion. That evening I felt I spoke with authority, although everything was difficult. I humbled myself before the people without telling them what had been my greatest problem during the whole week. When I told my host I would leave at eleven o'clock that night and that the Baptist pastor would take me to the next place, he was furious. "I will take you myself tomorrow!" But I knew that I had to do my own will now. At eleven o'clock I went out of the front door with my luggage and I found the Baptist minister there. That nocturnal journey was a joy. It was a present from the Lord. The minister told me what had happened in his congregation: "There were so many disagreements, so much hatred, that the Holy Spirit must have been very grieved with such a congregation, but almost all the members of my church have been in your meetings every evening and the Lord has worked! Tonight everything has altered. After the meeting we all stood outside, because we were not allowed to stay inside, and there we prayed together. People who have not been speaking to each other for years have now been reconciled. They have confessed their sins, they have put everything right. What happened there in front of the church was such a blessing that we know we can now start afresh with our whole congregation. We praise and thank the Lord that He brought you here. He used the whole week."

So it had not been wrong as I had feared. It had been difficult, but not for nothing! We had a joyful journey that dark night. From time to time he stopped the car and we had a time of prayer. I confessed my sin before the Lord. I wanted to start the work in the next place cleansed and sanctified. I had to confess to the Lord that I had been hurt in my pride, that I had had self-pity, that I was discouraged and had a critical spirit in my heart. The spirit of sorrow had been on the throne. What a joy to bring everything to the Lord, because when we confess our sins, He is faithful and just to forgive us our sins and the blood of Jesus cleanses us from all sins! This experience had been an exercise to get smaller. I had made a mistake when, in my enthusiasm, I offered too quickly to go to that mental institution. We must not make plans if we are not in the presence of the Lord. That is why prayer time gives the best atmosphere to plan a programme.

Once I read a legend: Peter and the other disciples of Jesus went with the Lord on a long journey. Everything went too slowly for Peter and he walked on alone. Then he came to a road where it was dangerous because of wild animals and robbers. Peter found himself in danger. He hid behind a rock and waited until the others came. Then he said to Jesus: "I was afraid; I was in danger. There are wild animals and robbers here." Jesus looked at him very kindly and said: "Peter, you must never go ahead of Me. You must always remain by My side, then you are safe."

7. VICTORY THROUGH THE BLOOD OF JESUS

"Now they have conquered him through the blood of the Lamb, and through the Word to which they bore witness. They did not cherish life even in the face of death!" (Rev. 12:11, Phillips).

Yes, the blood of Jesus Christ has great power!

There is perhaps not a word in the Bible that is so full of secret truths as the blood of Jesus. It is the secret of His incarnation, when Jesus took our flesh and blood; the secret of His obedience unto death, when He gave His blood at the Cross of Calvary; the secret of His love that went beyond all understanding, when He bought us with His blood; the secret of His victory over the enemy and the secret of our eternal salvation. Why does the devil hate this word? Because it reminds him of his defeat on Calvary by the death of Jesus who gave His blood for us, but also it reminds him of Jesus' life, the resurrected One, to whom we always may come with our sins. That is why the devil is afraid of it. The blood of Jesus Christ has great power.

Once I visited a big prison in Manila. It was a hotbed of sin. There were seven thousand prisoners. I had an opportunity to speak there during three afternoons and when I entered I noticed that above the door was written: "Security limit". I asked what that meant and was told that when anyone entered this prison he had to go at his own risk in the midst of a big group of criminals, because there were only a very few guards. I looked into my heart to see if I was afraid—and yes, I must admit that indeed there was much fear! But, what could I do? I knew that I was in the way of the Lord, so must obey! When I came to the inner court, a great surprise was waiting for me: There was a band of musicians of about ninety men! When they saw me, they started to play: "There is power, power, wonder-working power in the precious blood of the Lamb!" All my fear disappeared. There is no reason to be afraid when a child of God is under the protection of the blood of the Lamb, the blood of Jesus. God gave us a very great blessing. Three times I reached seven thousand men with the help of a loudspeaker. I reached them with the rich Gospel, the glad tidings for sinners.

8. VICTORY THROUGH THE NAME OF JESUS

"These signs will follow those who do believe: they will drive out evil spirits in my name ... they will lay their hands upon the sick and they will recover" (Mark 16:17,18, Phillips).

The name of Jesus is wonderful! Once I heard a story of a sick lady in Germany. A friend asked her: "Do you know it is written in the Bible that Jesus said: 'They will lay their hands upon the sick and they will recover'?" Then he read Mark 16 and asked "Do you believe the Bible?" "Yes," she said, "I believe the whole Bible." Then he simply did it. In the name of Jesus he laid his hands on her and she was healed. She was so happy that she went to her pastor and said: "Did you know that that text in Mark 16:18, is in the Bible?" The pastor's answer was: "I am so sorry, but I must tell you that that part of Mark 16 was added to the Bible long,

long afterwards." One moment she was very disappointed, but suddenly her eyes started to beam with joy and she said: "What a wonderful Book is the Bible, that even an added promise has so much power that I was healed!"

Yes, when we believe the rich treasures of the Bible, we experience that God, who gave us all these promises, really keeps them. The name of Jesus is a wonderful name. The Bible does not only teach us that we *can* pray in this name, but that we *should* pray in Jesus' name. Once I heard a very good example of this from my friend William Nagenda, an African brother. He told me about a letter that his wife wrote him when he was abroad. Their little boy aged three asked: "Mummy, what are you doing?" "I am writing a letter to Daddy." "I will write a letter to Daddy too." She gave him a piece of paper and a pencil and then he made all kinds of scrawls. "This is my letter to Daddy," the boy said. The mother wrote under all these scrawls: "This is Christopher's letter to his daddy." When William took this letter from the envelope, he first wanted to throw it away, but then he saw what was written on it: "This is Christopher's letter to his daddy." Suddenly he felt very proud and he asked his friend: "Have you a boy of three?" "Yes." "Has he ever written you a letter?" "No, of course not." "My son has written me a letter," and he showed him the paper with all the scrawls. He was very proud. Why did he set so much value on that letter? Because his wife had explained what those scrawls meant.

When we pray, it doesn't matter whether it is a beautiful prayer, or a prayer from our prayer book, or perhaps just a cry of distress directly to the Lord. It is never good enough for the holy God; but when we say: "In the name of Jesus," then it is just as if Jesus says: "Father, this is a prayer from your child, Mary, John, Charles ...", and then the heavenly Father is delighted with our prayer! That prayer is sanctified by the name of Jesus. Therefore, use this name! Not the name "Christ"; that is His title. The name that is above every name in heaven or on earth is the name: Jesus, Saviour! He is our strength. "In no one else can salvation be found. For in all the world no other name has been given to men but this, and it is by this name that we must be saved!" (Acts 4:12, Phillips).

That name brings heaven and earth together. One cannot overestimate the value of that name in the great final battle.

9. VICTORY THROUGH THE FULNESS
OF THE HOLY SPIRIT

"You are to be given power when the Holy Spirit has come to you. You will be witnesses to me, not only in Jerusalem, not only throughout Judaea, not only in Samaria, but to the very ends of the earth!" (Acts 1:8, Phillips).

This power of the Holy Spirit is of tremendous value to us. The Bible says: "Be filled with the Spirit!" In Harlem lived a woman who started a prayer meeting in her room. Her brother had not much faith about it and said: "You will never succeed!" But the day after, she told him: "My room was full up!" "All right, but just wait and see what happens next week!" But the next time she said: "My room was even fuller." And the third time: "Now it was fuller still!" Her brother said: "That is impossible; when your room is full, it cannot be fuller." "Oh yes," she said. "Every week we took some more furniture out of the room." When we are filled with the Holy Spirit, then another step may be necessary. It is possible that some furniture must be removed from the heart: television, or some books, friendships, personal hobbies; everything that can hinder us from following Jesus Christ. We can clear out still more for Jesus, so that we can give more room to the Holy Spirit. My glove cannot do anything by itself, but when my hand is in the glove, it can do a great deal. It can even cook, write and do many things! I know that it is not the glove, but the hand in the glove. When I put only one finger in the glove, then it cannot do anything! So it is with us. We are gloves; the Holy Spirit is the hand which can do everything, but we must give Him room right into the outer corners of our lives. Then we can expect that He can do a lot in and through us. In John 14:17 it is written: "He is with you now and will be in your hearts!" (Phillips). "So, if you, for all your evil, know how to give good things to your children, how much more likely is it that your heavenly Father will give the Holy Spirit to those who ask him!" (Luke 11:13, Phillips).

John the Baptist had said already: "The one who comes after me ... will baptise you with the Holy Spirit and with fire" (Matt. 3:11 N.E.B.). Jesus is the Baptiser in the Holy Spirit and therefore the fulness of the Holy Spirit is the birthright of every child of God.

Gifts of the Spirit

"Desire spiritual gifts" (1 Cor. 14:1).

A missionary in China had to endure brainwashing. He resisted and fought against it, but the moment came when he felt he was at the end of his strength. Then he started to pray in tongues. That fellowship with the Lord, in absolute relaxation, was his salvation. The enemy could not influence his mind any longer. I believe that the Lord has given this gift at this time to many of His children in many different churches and groups, be-

cause it is a strong weapon and will prove to be so in
the final battle. It is a fact that nothing has received so
much criticism and opposition, even among believing
Christians, as has this gift, which is described so clearly
in the Word of God. Paul says in 1 Cor. 14:5 (Phillips):
"I should indeed like you all to speak with tongues."
The "God is dead" theology and occultism, which are
practised even by Christians, receive less criticism and
resistance, yes, and even enmity, than this gift from the
Spirit. Mother Basilea, the leader of the "Sisters of
Mary" in Darmstadt, has said:

"We need the fulness of the Holy Spirit for the end-
time, which is the period in which the promise for the
Church will be more fully realised. The Church needs
in a much stronger degree the powers and the gifts of
the Holy Spirit operating in the battle against the sa-
tanic powers, against the Antichrist himself. That is
why there is given a special promise of the Holy Spirit
for the end-time. In the prophecies of the Old Testament, the coming of the Holy Spirit on earth and for
the people of Israel was a special sign of the end-time.
Of this time it is written: 'Until the Spirit be poured
upon us from on high ...' (Isa. 32:15). 'And it shall
come to pass in the last days, that I will pour out my
Spirit upon all flesh' (Joel 2:28; Acts 2:17). We cannot comprehend how the Holy Spirit works and acts.
He even gives gifts to people who have only just accepted Jesus as their Saviour. He continues to work in
their hearts and He sees to it that these gifts will be
used in the right way by bringing them into a healthy
inward attitude, step by step, until the image of Jesus
Christ is formed in us. He equips us with gifts and
power. He also sees to it, as we read in the Book of
Acts, that we humble ourselves over and over again
and fight against sin. He creates burning desire within

us, to follow after *agape* love more and more, and to achieve the full power of Jesus Christ through this inner attitude of the Spirit, in love. All this we owe to the Holy Spirit, who in His grace grants us these gifts; who leads us, admonishes us and convinces us; who wages war in us against the flesh; who prays and pleads. He is the life-giving Spirit, who renews us and fills our lives with prayer, and with fire to be His witnesses and to confess Jesus Christ.

The Gifts of the Holy Spirit in this time

"In the Acts of the Apostles we see that the kingdom of God, the Church of Jesus Christ, was built through the work of the Holy Spirit, His fruit and His gifts. The Word of God shows us that there is no substitute for the gifts of the Spirit. They were not only for that time, but also for today. The good Shepherd will give to His own a life which reveals His Spirit and power. For this equipment is necessary for the life of the Church, in her battle against the powers of darkness now, as in those days. Through the gifts, the Head of the Body gives power to its members, to resist deceiving spirits in every form. Also at this time, He gives her the gift of discernment of spirits, when new and deceiving powers are threatening the Church. He also gives her the gift of faith and of the working of miracles, when we stand today threatened by nuclear war. When the evidence of the unfolding of the power of the Antichrist becomes visible, then the Lord gives to His Church, through the gift of wisdom, the right word for this situation. The first Christian church, which was brought to life in an unusual way through the creating power of the Holy Spirit, needed the gifts of the Spirit to be built up. How much more do we need the gifts of the Spirit in this time in our churches and groups, where life is so often absent! One appeals to tradition and habits and refuses to acknowledge the truth which the Bible teaches us: 'The Spirit of God alone can give life to the soul' (2 Cor. 3:6). But this Spirit does not reveal Himself apart from the gifts of grace. The 'letter', as the apostle writes, that is to say, pious human effort to understand and grasp the Word of God, cannot be a substitute for these. Only the Spirit can give light. Only He can touch the heart. Only He can lead us to repentance, humility and reconciliation. The Spirit alone makes us understand the signs of the times and He shows us that we have to stand in the gap for a world that is doomed to destruction.

"Only the life-giving Spirit who gives His gifts can prepare the Church for the coming of the Lord. Real church life, as we see it in the Book of Acts, is inconceivable without the work of the Holy Spirit and His gifts. For the believers in the first church this was self-evident, because they had all received the Holy Spirit. And why should it be any different today? The New Testament considers the functioning of the gifts of the Spirit as an organic result and a self-evident phenomenon accompanying the receiving and working of the Holy Spirit. In the Bible you cannot find one single place that gives us any indication that the gifts of the Spirit were only necessary for the apostolic times. The slow 'drying up' of the stream of the gifts of the Spirit in the post-apostolic period (there has always been a little trickle) is not in accordance with the Biblical and historical plan of God's salvation. We must seek the reason for this in lack of faith and in the backsliding of the Church. Lack of alertness, obedience and faith can make it impossible for Christ to speak as intimately and as wonderfully as 'in the days of her youth' (Hosea 2:15).

"The gifts of the Spirit have a function which cannot be replaced by anything else. The gifts are a sign of a further penetrating work of Christ, out of the matchlessness of eternity into this poor world. Since the triune God has been declared dead by some, we need evidence that He lives! People must be confronted today with the reality of the Holy Spirit, who in truth glorifies the Father and the Son, when He gives people His gifts, such as the gifts of faith, of working miracles and of healing, in love; for through these the greatness and the omnipotence of God shines as a light. Testimonies of the life of the Holy Spirit in the Church of Jesus Christ are very necessary today. Therefore we need men and women who are full of the Spirit, in whom the gifts of grace are active. Such people can show the world that God is alive. Also through the gifts of healing, Jesus glorifies Himself today. Jesus once performed miracles of healing to show that the power and the works of the devil are destroyed, and that His kingdom is coming: 'He went about doing good and healing all who suffered from the devil's power—because God was with him' (Acts 10:38, Phillips).

"This gift of healing is promised to all who believe in Him (Mark 16:18), and particularly to the elders. We must always be prepared to lay on hands (Jas. 5:14), because as a matter of fact every sick person in the church has to be brought first to Jesus, for He says: 'Come unto me, all ye that labour and are heavy laden.'

"So we must measure the value of the gifts in accordance with what is written in Holy Scripture, where they are shown to be important. We must not measure their value incorrectly, or underestimate their importance, because in some cases they have been misused. There have also been false prophets, and sometimes there has been the misuse of the gifts of healing and of tongues. To question or deny their value would be denying the evidence of the Bible. When the Holy Scripture says: 'Desire spiritual gifts' (1 Cor. 14:1), then we cannot substitute for it 'Keep away from the gifts of the Spirit', or 'Fight against them', simply because there have been false prophets and prophecies which have possibly been straight from the devil. We can only fight against the misuse, never against the gifts themselves.

"What a responsibility! God offers to His Church these gifts, but on condition that we must pray for them. Very often we do not do that, and therefore we are so poor and in want. So we become guilty of the lives of many people who perhaps could have found the way to Jesus, if the gifts had been active. For God uses not only the preaching of the Word, but He also uses today all the gifts which the Word of God promises us, so that He will be glorified by them, the Church built up, and those who stand far off come to believe in Him. This also applies to the gift of speaking in tongues. Should the Holy Spirit, who is still the same, suddenly let one of His gifts of grace disappear, when Jesus Himself mentioned it as one of the signs that should follow believers? It is just this gift, which gives us words to worship Him, when the words of our human language are not sufficient, because the glory and the love of God are so great, that our mother tongue does not have the words to express it. But the Holy Spirit Himself 'maketh intercession for us with groanings which cannot be uttered' (Rom. 8:26). He, who is the only One who can fathom the depths of God, gives us words of adoration of the all-mighty, holy, eternal God, whose Being we can never understand. We praise Him in these new tongues, languages which are given through the Spirit."

Thus Mother Basilea has spoken. And what joy that the Holy Spirit gives us even God's own love in our hearts (Rom 5:5), for gifts without love are nothing.

"If I speak with the eloquence of men and of angels, but have no love, I become no more than blaring brass or crashing cymbal. If I have the gift of foretelling the future and hold in my mind not only all human knowledge but the very secrets of God, and if I also have that absolute faith which can move mountains, but have no love, I amount to nothing at all. If I dispose of all that I possess, yes, even if I give my own body to be burned, but have no love, I achieve precisely nothing" (1 Cor. 13:1—3, Phillips).

10. VICTORY THROUGH YIELDING

"Who shall also confirm you unto the end, that ye may be blameless in the day of our Lord Jesus Christ" (1 Cor. 1:8).

Are you prepared for the coming of Jesus? Am I prepared for the coming of Jesus? It is so wonderful that it is written so clearly in the Bible—it is only by full surrender that we are made ready for His coming again. If it depended on us, then one day we would be successful, but the next day just the opposite. William Nagenda, an evangelist from Uganda, has given us a very good example of what surrender means. He told that one day he arrived home after a long trip. There his little son of three stood at the station waiting for him. "Daddy, I will carry your suitcase," he said. William did not want to disappoint him and said: "All right, put your hand on my hand." So they went on their way and the little boy kept his weak little hand on the strong hand of his father. They came home and the little boy said:

"Mummy, I carried Daddy's suitcase." So it is with us. Our hands are not strong enough, but when we lay our weak hand on the strong hand of Jesus, then He Himself prepares us for His coming again. We must not forget "that the One who has begun his good work in you will go on developing it until the day of Jesus Christ" (Phil. 1:6, Phillips).

We shall not be so ignorant as the little boy and say: "I carried the suitcase!" We shall honour the Lord for all this. We shall see Jesus face to face, and it is important whether we shall see Him as our judge or as our Redeemer. Have you put your weak hand on the strong hand of your Saviour? Do you believe that Jesus can help you? Paul says: "For I *know* the One in whom I have placed my confidence, and I am perfectly certain that the work he has committed to me is safe in his hands until that day" (2 Tim 1:12, Phillips).

There is still a tremendous struggle and fight, but the moment comes when our sanctification is complete. In 1 Thess. 3:12,13 (Phillips) it is written that this will really happen: "May the Lord give you the same increasing and overflowing love for each other and towards all men as we have towards you. May he establish you, holy and blameless in heart and soul, before God, the Father of us all." Yes, the best is yet to be! One day there will be an end to the battle. Then there will be the victory, victory through Jesus Christ! "May the God of peace make you holy through and through. May you be kept in soul and mind and body in spotless integrity until the coming of our Lord Jesus Christ" (1 Thess. 5:23, Phillips).

Full surrender includes also our mistakes and errors. Once, somebody visited a weavers' school. He asked one of the pupils: "What do you do when you have made a mistake? Can you cut it out, or must you start again from the very beginning?" The pupil said: "No, our teacher is such a great artist that when we make a mis-

take, he uses that to increase the beauty of the pattern."
That is what Jesus does with us! Our feeling of inferiority is really pride, because we will not accept that our
ability is limited. We want to be better than we really
are.

But it is so wonderful that when we acknowledge our
mistakes, the Lord sometimes uses them to His honour.
I remember that when I was in Japan the first time, I
had the problem that to me most Japanese looked alike.
That lasted about a month. One finds that when a Japanese comes to our country, he thinks the same. But I
found it difficult. Once I had to lead a Bible study
group for students. During the meeting I saw someone
entering the room. I thought: "Oh, that is the director
of the Bible School!" But he was not; he was a professor
of a non-Christian university. When I had finished my
talk I asked this man: "Will you close this meeting with
prayer?" The professor was startled: "I have never
prayed before." Then I saw my mistake. I recognised
him and said: "Oh, that does not matter; I will do it,
Professor." But Japanese people are very polite and after the meeting he came to me, bowed very deeply and
said: "I am so sorry that I could not comply with your
request, but I do not know how to pray." "I have a
great deal of respect for you, Professor, because you
have not done it. If you had been a superficial man,
then perhaps you might have said a prayer without believing it. It was very good that you did not do it."
Then I asked: "But why are you not a Christian?"
"Then I should first have to study Christianity." "It is
not written in my Bible: 'To him who studies Christianity God gives power to become a child of God,' but
'Those who receive Jesus, he gives them the power to
become a child of God' (John 1:12) ."

Then I started to show him the way of salvation. But
while I preached the gospel to him, I prayed quietly in

my heart. Someone who is counselling must always have at the same moment the "horizontal and the vertical connection" at work. After half an hour this professor came to the decision that made the angels in heaven rejoice, the decision for Jesus! Here you see how the Lord used the mistake of foolish Corrie ten Boom to give this man the opportunity to be saved for eternity. This professor had a strategically important position in the University of Tokyo. Of course, we cannot make a system of this. Not everyone who goes to India discovers America! But by all means we must lay our failures in the hands of the Lord. When there is total surrender, then we walk relaxed at the hand of the Saviour.

3

EQUIPMENT FOR ACTIVE SERVICE

11. LOVE

"The love of God is shed abroad in our hearts by the Holy Ghost which is given unto us" (Rom. 5:5).

WHEN I WAS IN A CONCENTRATION CAMP during the last war, we had to stand every day for two or three hours for roll-call, often in the icy-cold wind. That was something terrible. Once a woman guard used these hours to demonstrate her cruelty. I could hardly bear to see and hear what happened in front of me. Suddenly a skylark started to sing high in the sky. We all looked up, and when I looked to the sky and listened to its song, I looked still higher and thought of Psa. 103:11 (R.S.V.): "For as the heavens are high above the earth, so great is his steadfast love toward those who fear him." Suddenly I saw that this love of God was a greater reality than the cruelty that I experienced myself and saw around me. "Oh the love of God, how deep and great, far deeper than man's deepest hate." God sent that skylark every day for three weeks, just at the time of roll-call, to give us an opportunity to turn away our eyes from the cruelty of men to the ocean of God's love. This love is a protection as well as a weapon. It guards us against impatience, against zeal without sense, against annoyance, against bitterness, against gloating. It is a very strong weapon in the battle to win souls, for it never gives in. It is slow to lose patience, it looks for a way of being constructive, it is glad with all good men when truth prevails. Love knows no limit to its endurance, no end to its trust, no fading of its hope: it can outlast anything. It is, in fact, the one thing that still stands when all else has fallen (1 Cor. 13).

How do we get that strong love? It is the Holy Spirit who gives us that love (Rom. 5:5).

The first love

When I had been wandering around the world as a "tramp of the Lord" for twenty years, I suddenly fell ill. The doctor said to me: "If you continue with this work, then you will stand it only for one more year; but if you go on furlough for a year, then you can perhaps work for another ten years." I consulted my "Employer", my Saviour, and He said very clearly that this advice of the doctor was in His plan. I could live during that "sabbath-year" in Lweza, a beautiful house in Uganda. It is a house with a nice park around it. The climate is ideal. Nature is so matchless. There one has a view from the garden over Lake Victoria. I could work there a little bit. There are many universities, churches, prisons and groups in Kampala, the nearby town. So, with two or three meetings every week, my spirit remained active. But sleeping every night in the same bed gave me a great rest during that time. During these last twenty years I have slept perhaps in more than a thousand different beds.

In November the "sabbath-year" had gone by. Conny, my fellow-worker, and I put the world map on my bed to make plans for a whole year. Our method is always the same; first we listen to what God's plan is and then we sign it. We will be "planned" by Him. It became a very good programme: three months in different countries in Africa, two months in America, three months in Eastern Europe behind the Iron Curtain. But my heart did not rejoice. When I was alone I said to the Lord: "I prefer to stay here. There is so much to do in Kampala and Entebbe, the two nearest cities. I will work for You, I am willing to have meetings every day, pastoral care, writing books, but please, let me sleep every night in the same bed. Everyone can understand that I, at my age, should take it a bit easier." I was then seventy-three. This new plan of mine made me really happy.

Then Conny called me; there was a visitor. It was an African minister from Ruanda. He started immediately to welcome me: "We are so glad that you are willing to come to Ruanda again. Five years ago you helped us so marvellously when you told what the Lord had been to you in your great need. You said at that time: 'It was not my faith that helped me through three prisons. My faith was weak and was often wavering. It was the Lord Himself who carried me through. He promised: "I am with you all the days." I have always believed, but now I know from experience that Jesus' light is stronger than the deepest darkness. It is good that I can tell you that. If you should meet great difficulties, then you could say: "I have not Corrie ten Boom's faith," but when it is Jesus, then you can trust that the same Saviour who helped Corrie ten Boom will also carry you through.'" The African brother continued: "That was all very interesting to me, but I had never been in prison. For many of us it was just a bit of theory, but in these last five years there has been civil war in our country. Many of us have been in prison. I myself was for two years in a cell. Then we remembered everything you had said and it was a great comfort to us. That is why we are so happy that you are now coming again to Ruanda."

But I was not happy at all. His words were different

from what I wanted. It is always good in such a situation to ask a question yourself. Then you can lead the conversation in another direction. That is why I asked: "How is the church in Ruanda? What kind of message do they need now?" Without hesitating one moment the brother opened his Bible and read:

"Write this to the angel of the Church in Ephesus: These words are spoken by the one who holds the seven stars safe in his right hand, and who walks among the seven golden lampstands. I know what you have done; I know how hard you have worked and what you have endured. I know that you will not tolerate wicked men, that you have put to the test self-styled 'apostles', who are nothing of the sort, and have found them to be liars. I know your powers of endurance—how you have suffered for the sake of my name and have not grown weary. But I hold this against you, that you do not love as you did at first. Remember then how far you have fallen. Repent and live as you lived at first. Otherwise, if your heart remains unchanged, I shall come to you and remove your lampstand from its place" (Rev. 2:1–6, Phillips).

This arrow penetrated my heart. Not only Ruanda, not only the church of Ephesus, but also Corrie ten Boom needed this message! I had lost my first love. Twenty years before I had come out of a concentration camp, starved, weak, but in my heart there was a burning love; love for the Lord, who had carried me through so faithfully; love for the people around me, a longing to tell them—Jesus is a reality, He lives, He is Victor, I know it from experience! I went to Germany and lived in the midst of ruins. I was interested in winning souls for eternity, to glorify the Lord, so that everyone should hear: we can never fall so deeply, always deeper are the everlasting arms that carry us.

Yes, that was at that time, and now? Now I was interested in my bed. I had lost my first love. Then I read Rev. 2:5b, " ... except thou repent." Suddenly joy came in my heart. I saw that the door to repentance was wide open! I coud bring my sin, my cold heart, to Him who is faithful and just (1 John 1:7,9) . I did it; I confessed my sins and asked for forgiveness. And then happened what always happens when we bring a sin to God in the name of Jesus: He forgave me. Jesus cleansed my heart with His blood, and a heart which is cleansed by the blood of Jesus, He fills with the Holy Spirit. The fruit of the Spirit is love! Not my first love, but a much greater; God's love was poured out into my heart. I went again on my journeys. What a great joy it was to experience the love of God, who gave me rivers of living water for the thirsty world of Africa, America and Eastern Europe. Of course, it can be the will of God that old people retire from their work, and in great thankfulness to the Lord enjoy their pensions, but for me the way of obedience is to travel on, although not as much as before.

The doctor has allowed me to work for seventy per cent of the time. In this time we must be vigilant. Jesus has warned us in Matt. 24: 12 that the love of most men waxes cold, because iniquity abounds. It is very easy to belong to the "most men", but the gate of conversion is wide open. Hallelujah!

Love for the Enemy

When Jesus tells us to love our enemies, He Himself gives us the love that He demands from us.

In Africa I visited the cell of a young man who was sentenced to death. His hands were chained and his dark skin had many red wounds, caused by lashes. Behind me stood three soldiers. The cell was absolutely empty; only a plank on the floor and high up in the wall a very little window. The prisoner looked very healthy and strong. The tragedy that this man had to die overwhelmed me.

I sat down beside him and prayed for a word from the Lord. "Have you ever heard of the Cross of Jesus Christ, where He carried the sins of the whole world, also your sins?" He nodded. "Do you believe in Jesus Christ, that He will be your Saviour too?" "Yes, I love Him, but I have not always been faithful. Politics have taken up my time and attention completely, but now I have brought all my sins to Jesus. He has forgiven me. If I may live any longer, then I will serve Him with all my life." "Have you forgiven the people that have brought you here, who have your death on their conscience?" "No, I hate them." "I can understand that. I will tell you one of my experiences.

"During the war in Holland, I helped to save Jewish people, because Hitler wanted to kill them. One day a man came to me, who told me that his wife had also helped the Jews and that now she had been arrested. 'She is in the police station and probably she will be put to death. Now there is a policeman who is willing to let her escape, if we pay him six hundred guilders, but I have no money.' 'I can help you,' I said. 'Come back in an hour.' In the meantime I collected all the money from my friends and all I had myself, and it was exactly six hundred guilders. I gave it to him to save the life of his wife. But he was a betrayer. His wife was not arrested at all. The enemy had told him to find out whether I helped Jewish people. So this man thought that at the same time he could make some money out of this situation. He went home with six hundred guilders in his pocket. But five minutes later the enemy came and my whole family was arrested. Later, when I heard that this man had betrayed us, hatred came into my heart, just as it happened with you. I had given him the last money that I had. But then I read in the Bible that hatred is really murder in God's eyes (Matt. 5:21,22).

"How glad I was that I knew what I could do against hatred. 'If we confess our sins, the blood of Jesus Christ His Son cleanseth us from all sin. He is faithful and just to forgive us our sins, and to cleanse us from all unrighteousness' (1 John 1:7,9). I brought my hatred to Jesus. He forgave me and cleansed my heart with His blood. After the war this betrayer was sentenced to death. I wrote to him: 'What you have done through your betrayal caused the death of my eighty-four-year-old father, my brother, his son and my sister in prison. I myself have terribly suffered through your fault, but I have forgiven you everything. This is just a very little example of the forgiveness and love of Jesus. He lives in my heart, that is why I can forgive you. Jesus will also come into your heart and will make you a child of God. Confess your sins to Him. On the Cross of Calvary He has finished all for your sins and mine.' Later he wrote me: 'I have prayed: "Jesus, when You can give such a love for the enemy in the heart of someone who follows You, then there is hope for me." I have indeed confessed my sins to Him. Now I know that I am a child of God, cleansed by the blood of Jesus.'

"So you see that Jesus used me to save the soul of this same man I had hated so much. Do you know that if you do not forgive, you yourself do not receive forgiveness? Jesus said: 'For if you forgive other people their failures, your heavenly Father will also forgive you. But if you will not forgive other people, neither will your heavenly Father forgive you your failures' (Matt. 6:14–16, Phillips). You cannot do that, neither can I, but Jesus can!" The same day the prisoner sent a message to his wife: "Forgive my murderers. You are not able to do it, I am not able, but Jesus is able. If we are not willing, then we ourselves do not receive forgiveness."

When Jesus comes and we have bitterness, yes, even hatred in our hearts, then we are not ready to meet Him with a clean heart: "Everyone who has at heart a hope like that keeps himself pure, for he knows how pure Christ is" (1 John 3:3, Phillips).

In the time of the final battle, many will be filled with hatred. If we are not cleansed from bitterness, then we do not stand on victory ground. It is very easy to belong to the masses of people. It is one of the laws of the Kingdom of God that men receive peace only if they are always ready to forgive unreservedly. We never touch the love of God so much as when we love our enemies. "The love of God is shed abroad in our hearts by the Holy Ghost which is given unto us" (Rom. 5:5). He does the job. Hallelujah!

12. FELLOWSHIP OF THE SAINTS

"Make sure that your everyday life is worthy of the gospel of Christ. So that ... I may know that you are standing fast in a united spirit, battling with a single mind for the faith of the gospel" (Phil. 1:27, Phillips).

When there is no unity in an army, one cannot expect victory. We need the fellowship of the saints. The fruit of the Spirit of Gal. 5:22 makes the fellowship of the children of God a joyful possibility. In this battle it is very essential that we are one in spirit with the other soldiers in the army of Jesus Christ.

We do not need to agree with each other about all doctrines, but through the gift of discernment of the spirits we can find out with whom we can be united in the battle and with whom we cannot. I believe that the Lord is willing to give at this time the discernment of the spirits to his children, because it is a necessary part of our armour. We *must* be able to discern the spirits. That is why the Holy Spirit equips us with this power. The Bible tells us that in this time many will try to deceive us, yes, if it were possible, even the very elect (Matt. 24:24).

I am so glad that there is written: "If it were possible." Yes, the Lord protects us from the great danger of being deceived. It is the Holy Spirit who gives us the love and the wisdom to have discernment of the spirits instead of criticism. Criticism is a great danger in our country. Loveless criticism by a believer nearly ruins the other believer being criticised. But on the other hand, we must clearly discern what is from the devil and what is from the Holy Spirit. We have to exercise ourselves. The devil is not always a roaring lion; he can also be very "pious", and then it is difficult to discern. But it is such a joy that we have a "blank cheque". In Jas. 1:5 (Phillips) is written: "And if any of you does not know how to meet any particular problem he has only to ask God—who gives generously to all men without making them feel foolish or guilty—and he may be quite sure that the necessary wisdom will be given him." He gives it. So we can go through life as wise people, because His wisdom gives us open ears and eyes.

By the fruit we know the tree. If there is confusion and lovelessness and a spirit of criticism, then we know that the enemy has been busy. But if there is love, if there is a longing to save souls, if there is spiritual activity and joy in prayer and Bible-reading, then we know that the Holy Spirit has been at work. "If we really are living in the same light in which He eternally exists, then we have true fellowship with each other" (1 John 1:7, Phillips).

As soon as we come in contact with other people, we detect the weak points of ourselves and of the others, and then it is such a joy that at the end of this text is written: "The blood which He shed for us keeps us clean from any and every sin." The finished work at the Cross is our salvation. When Jesus died there, He carried the sins of the whole world. That is why we can bring our sins directly to Him and He cleanses us. When the blood of Jesus cleanses us, He does it completely. We can walk in the light because He is in the light, and not because we have the light in ourselves.

You and I can walk in the light, because Jesus lives, because Jesus is Victor and because we can expect all from Him. We are like the moon, not like the sun. The sun has light from itself, the moon only reflects the light. God educates us through our fellowship with others.

Sometimes we need a little grindstone to polish our character. By nature my heart is proud. Besides this, all over the world so much love is shown to me and I am held in high esteem by so many everywhere, that there is a great danger of becoming "somebody". Then I must decrease, and therefore the Lord uses fellow-Christians. I had started a work for which I had a great love in my heart, but my friends who in fact carried out this work for me because I was always travelling, could not agree with the aim and with my way of bringing the gospel. Then they asked me to withdraw and to give them a free hand. I became angry and bitterness came into my heart. I confessed it immediately to the Lord and He took it away; I could forgive my friends. But during the night I awoke and my first thought was how had it been possible that my friends had been so unkind, had behaved almost like enemies. Then I saw that in fact my heart was not yet free. Again I immediately confessed it to the Lord. I thought I had the victory, but the next night it came again. Is this because one does not carry the armour of God consciously during the night? Does the enemy know that when we are asleep we are not ready for battle? It is necessary that in the evening before we go to sleep our whole being and also our subconsciousness is cleansed and that we fully surrender to Him so that there is not a single starting-point left for the enemy.

I complained about it to the Lord: "Why am I still so angry? I have experienced that You gave me grace to forgive even those who murdered my family during the war. I have always been able to preach to other people that when You tell us to love our enemies, You give us the love that You require from us. Why is there still bitterness in my heart? Lord, when I remember how often You have forgiven me in more than seventy years of my life, why is it difficult for me to forgive this? Lord, this is a problem, for I know that if I do not forgive, You will not forgive me." Then I became quiet.

That same day I heard a good illustration. When someone has been ringing the church bells—bim bam— bim bam—there comes the moment when he stops, no matter whether it is done electrically or by hand. But after that there often comes another bim-bam, then again a bim, then again a bam, and perhaps still a few times more. But he does not worry about that, because he knows that there has come an end to the bell-ringing, and very soon the bim-bams will stop. So it is also with the bitterness one has brought to the Lord. Bim-bams can come back, but then we must simply bring them again to the Lord. He is Victor, and soon He makes it possible by the Holy Spirit that instead of being annoyed, we love those who have sinned against us. When other people make it hard for us, then we must pray that the Lord will use this for our sanctification. Pray for them and love them as the Holy Spirit in us loves them. Then this becomes a practical training for the victory of the final battle. This experience has helped me to counsel many other people who had to resist the same temptations. I was not able to do it, but Jesus was Victor. He gave it to me. That helped them to turn their eyes in the right direction to look on high. I have learned still more. I have seen that my heart was too much tied to this work. I would not give in because my sister Betsie had inspired me to start it, for what God had told her at that time in the concentration camp had become my mission later on.

So I had to learn not to live out of the past, but to be obedient to the vocation I had to fulfil now. The Lord also sets us free from the bonds of the good past. If we will follow Jesus in all things, then we go the way of the Cross and this includes too that very often we are not understood even by our own friends. The Lord gives grace to be able to accept fully this being misunderstood. When I get bitter feelings against my friends, then I pray to the Lord Jesus to take up my thoughts. In my imagination I have a talk with Him and my friends together. Then He gives His love and peace, and all bitterness disappears out of my heart. This experience has made me richer and stronger.

When Jesus was arrested there were three reactions among the disciples. Peter hit out and the ear of Malchus was cut off; several disciples ran away; John remained behind with Jesus and suffered with Him. Cross-bearing means: to suffer with Jesus. So we may fill up in our daily lives that which is behind of the afflictions of Christ in our flesh (Col. 1:24). It is not my job to persuade my friends, only the Holy Spirit convicts of sins. We have only to deal with our own sins and we must pray: "Search me, O God, and know my heart: try me, and know my thoughts: and see if there be any wicked way in me, and lead me in the way everlasting" (Psa. 139:23,24).

13. DEVOTION IN SERVICE

"I was in prison, and ye came unto me" (Matt. 25:36).

The time of training is a time of active service. When we know that we are in an important battle and also know that this battle will be victorious, then there is a radiance on all our daily adventures. These experiences need not be extraordinary, but one sees all kinds of work as a part of the victory and the building of the kingdom of God.

My father often said: "My name is on the shop, but it would be proper to have God's name on the window. I am a watchmaker by the grace of God. It is God's watchmaker's shop." When we start to see more or less everything from God's point of view, then we always seek and find opportunities to help others.

In Brazil lives a very simple woman. She loves the Lord. Her friends went every week to a women's prison to take the gospel through preaching, singing and counselling. She could not take part in this for she could not do such things, but she had love in her heart! One thing she knew very well—baking cakes. She suggested to her friends that she go with them and take a cake with her. I got an invitation to speak there and I will never forget it. All the women in this prison came. The beginning was not pleasant. We were searched by the guards, our bags were opened, they fingered our clothes in case we had hidden something. But after that the women who had come with me started to sing hymns and I brought the Word. Then, when we were through with everything the moment came that seemed to be the climax for the prisoners.

Our friend brought in the cake she had made. She had taken a knife with her and cut the cake in many little pieces. Then she had also brought along little pieces of paper in many different colours. Every piece of cake was nicely packed and offered to the women. In the love of her heart she had understood what colours mean for prisoners. It was a feast, a real feast; everyone was happy. People laughed, everyone was kind to one another and when we went, we left these women with a blessing in their hearts. Poor stranded lives, murderesses and thieves, but they had heard the Word of God and they had experienced the love of God through the kindness of this simple woman! Every week she does that and the women know and count on it, that after the preaching of the gospel this little treat comes too. Yes, everyone can work in this training time. This simple, faithful woman will one day hear: "I was in prison and you came to Me and gave Me cake."

Chain Reactions

In Australia I was at a very big meeting and at the end I invited the people who wanted to be saved to come forward. The first who came were two little girls. I had told the people that they could go to a room behind the altar, but these children had not understood that. They stopped in front of me, and one asked with a very clear little voice, so that everyone in the church heard: "Am I too small to ask Jesus to come into my heart?" "No, not at all. Jesus was interested even in sparrows and you are much bigger than a sparrow! Jesus said: 'Let the little children come unto me!' I myself was five years old when I asked Jesus to come into my heart and He came in and He has never left me." Then the little girl said aloud, so that the whole church could hear it: "Lord Jesus, I have been very naughty. Will You come into my heart and cleanse it with Your blood?" And Jesus came in.

That is what He said in Rev. 3:20: "Behold, I stand at the door, and knock: if any man hear my voice, and open the door, I will come in to him." And it is just as certain that He will come in, when you, who read this, open your heart's door to Him. He does not ask: "What is your age?" I said to the other girl: "Will you do the same?" Then the little one said: "I did it three weeks ago, and after that I prayed every day for Betty, and now Betty has done it!" "Then you must pray together for a third girl." They looked at each other very thoughtfully and said at the same moment: "Anne. That must be Anne!" And then they promised to pray for Anne, until the Lord would knock at her heart and when Anne had opened her heart for Jesus, they would pray together with Anne for a fourth girl and so on.

This is the chain reaction of the gospel which started in the hearts of two little girls, who were perhaps not yet eight years old. This chain reaction of intercession can start in everyone's heart, and so everyone can cooperate to prepare the coming of the Lord Jesus, now today!

Then there was the youth group in Invercargill to which I spoke. It was a tremendously blessed evening; the Holy Spirit worked in hearts. There were about thirty young people. A year later I came back. I met the minister and asked how his youth group was going on. "Oh," he said, "it goes very well. Will you please speak to them again? They meet tonight."

I went, but when I entered the hall, I said: "I will be very happy to bring a message here, but I had meant a different group. There are about two hundred young people here. I meant that group of thirty, but it does not matter at all." "But this *is* the same group," they said. "When the Holy Spirit began to work in our hearts, we got a real longing to win souls. One evening a week we came together for Bible study and intercession. Everyone could mention a name of a friend or someone who did not know the Lord yet. But then they had to speak to them about the Lord Jesus in the course of that same week. When that other person came to know the Lord, then he or she was invited to come also. But this person had sometimes three or four other people to pray for, and so it worked like a snowball that became bigger and bigger. Now there are more than two hundred. Several of them have gone to Bible School!"

What God can do with the life of one person who understands that he is a little part of the Kingdom of God, at a time in which we can expect that Jesus comes soon! God has a plan. The "fulness of the Gentiles" must come. And when the last of them comes to faith, then it is the fulness of time. Everyone who is used by the Lord to bring other people to Him co-operates to prepare the Second Coming of the Lord and to hasten it.

14. FAITHFULNESS

"When thou vowest a vow unto God, defer not to pay it; for he hath no pleasure in fools" (Eccl. 5:4).

To be a conqueror it is very important to remain faithful. It is good to ask yourself: "Did I ever vow to God, and then not keep it?" Have you ever been singing with your whole heart after an inspiring talk: "Take my life and let it be consecrated, Lord, to Thee. Take my silver and my gold; take my moments and my days ..."?

Have you ever said to the Lord: "I will go to the place where you send me, even to the mission field"? Did you then go to your work again without paying any attention to the marching-orders of the Master? Did you then allow that promise just to disappear out of your heart?

Have you ever promised to give your tithes to the Lord? Did you ever tell Him that you would never speak negatively about other people and never exaggerate? Have you ever said any of these things to the Lord and not done them? Then you are not faithful.

In Rev. 2:10 (R.S.V.) is written: "Be faithful unto death, and I will give you the crown of life."

In Judges 6 the story of Gideon begins. He was really very small even in his own eyes, but he received a mission from God and he did not dare do it. In verse 13 we read that there was rebellion in his heart. He complained and was without courage. He did not go at all. Then God said to him: "Go in this thy might." Gideon had feelings of inferiority. He made excuses. "My family is poor in Manasseh, and I am the least in my father's house."

Did you know that feeling inferior is pride, and that you are not willing to accept your limitations? God's answer was: "I am with you." Gideon had very little faith and said: "Show me a sign." He received it. Gideon was afraid and the Lord said: "Peace be unto you."

In Rev. 21 the fearful people are mentioned together with unbelievers, murderers, whoremongers, idolaters, etc. Cowardice is a sin that deserves judgment. When we continue to read the story of Gideon, we see that this little man destroyed the idol of his father, a very dangerous thing to do, as his fellow-townsmen could kill him for it. Then God commanded him to attack the enemy and his faith was tried. "But the Spirit of the Lord came upon Gideon and he blew a trumpet" (Judges 6:34). Gideon obeyed, and finally he overcame a whole army with a gang of three hundred men. How did that happen? Gideon had not a great faith, but he had faith in a great God.

The fruit of the Spirit is faithfulness. And for those who are in training for the final battle, the encouragement stands that God's faithfulness is for us. "Great is thy faithfulness" (Lam. 3:23).

Our faithfulness to God is the fruit of the Spirit. That becomes a quality in us only when we give room to the Holy Spirit in our hearts and lives. Be filled with God's Spirit, and faithfulness, the fruit of the Spirit, will be your portion.

God said to Gideon: "Go in this thy might." It is wonderful that God gives us His strength and that God's strength is demonstrated in our weakness.

I was in Argentina. One day I was asked to visit some patients in a hospital. There had been a terrible polio epidemic. For the first time in my life I saw people lying in iron lungs. The tragedy so overcame me that I could hardly bear it. A nurse asked me: "Will you speak with that Jewish man there?" He was not in an iron lung, but lay on a bed that went up and down. When his legs went up, his midriff pushed against his lungs and he could breathe out. When his legs went down, he could breathe in. He was fed by a little tube in his nose. He could not speak but he could write. When I looked at him I said in despair: "Oh Lord I cannot do this. Please let me go somewhere else, so that I can cry in a little corner. I am not able to speak to this man." When I say to the Lord: "I cannot do this," I always receive the answer: "I have known that for a long time, but it is good that you know it too, for now you can let Me do it." And I said: "Now Lord, then you do it." And He did. I could speak to this man. I showed him an embroidery, that on one side shows only a tangle of threads, but on the other a beautiful crown. I said: "When I see you lying on this bed I think of this embroidery. There has been a time in my life when it seemed like the tangled side of this crown. I saw no pattern, no beauty, no harmony. I was in prison, where my sister died before my eyes. But all that time I knew that God has no problems, only plans. There is never panic in heaven. Later on I saw God's side of the pattern. Because I have had to go through deep suffering in that prison, I was able to comfort people afterwards, because I could tell them: 'Jesus' light is stronger than the deepest darkness. When you have experienced the darkness of a concentration camp, you know how deep that darkness can be!' "

Then I spoke to him about the Messiah, Jesus, the Son of God, who died on the Cross for our sins. It seemed that when He died as if the whole plan of His life was broken, but just there He has given the answer to the problem of the sin of the whole world, for He has carried our punishment. And this Jesus did not only *die* for us, but He lives, for He is risen from the dead and He has said: "Lo, I am with you all the days—to the [very] close and consummation of the age" (Matt. 28:20, A.N.T.) . He will even live in our hearts. We may use His name, and pray in His name. And so I told him the happy message of Jesus' death and life. The man took a piece of paper and wrote: "I see already the beautiful side of the embroidery of my life."

What a victory it was for him to lie there, not being able to move, or speak or breathe, and in spite of all this, to see God's side. That was really a very great miracle. We had a good time together and I was so thankful. I could pray and then thank the Lord with him. The next day I went again to the hospital and asked the nurse: "May I speak with him again?" She told me that he had beckoned her, when I had left, and then wrote on his little writing pad: "For the first time in my life I have prayed in Jesus' name." Then he closed his eyes and died. This Jewish man had found Jesus in the last moment of his life. And God had used me for that when I was not able to do it. Yes, God's strength is demonstrated in our weakness.

When the marching orders of our King are given and seem very exacting, then we need not fear, for He Himself gives us the courage, the faithfulness and the strength to obey Him. "Go in this thy might," He says, when He has given us through the Holy Spirit the fruit of the Spirit, faithfulness and strength. "If we are faithless He always remains faithful. He cannot deny His own nature" (2 Tim. 2:13, Phillips).

15. FAITH

"Above all be sure you take faith as your shield, for it can quench every burning missile the enemy hurls at you" (Eph. 6:16, Phillips).

We are often in danger when we look at our own faith. But in Heb. 12:2 (Phillips) is written: "Let . . . our eyes (be) fixed on Jesus the source and goal of our faith." Before the war I had a watchmaker's shop. Sometimes it happened that a new watch I had in the shop did not run well. Then I did not repair it, but sent it back to the factory. When the manufacturer had repaired the watch it went exactly right.

When my faith does not work, when I am too busy with myself, then something is not right. But I do not think about repairing my faith myself. I do the same as I did with the watch. I send it back to the manufacturer. He only, the Lord who had made my faith, can renew it. When He has repaired it, then my faith works again. Here again we need to change the direction of our looking, away from our faith, unto Jesus.

Hudson Taylor, the great hero of faith, has said: "We do not need a great faith, but we need faith in a great

God." And this we have! The almighty God! Jesus speaks about a faith as small as a mustard seed and yet so dynamic that it can remove mountains. The Pharisees showed their faith; they carried it to the market-place, to the corners of the street, into the temple, so that everyone could see it, but their faith had no power, it was empty.

As we are ourselves, so our faith also is hidden with Jesus in God. That is what we have to learn. We are like fighters who are sent into the world, as into an arena, to fight in the strength of our faith and to conquer. Perhaps there is no other place where the change of direction of our looking is so necessary as just here. Look away from yourself and your faith; look to Him, the Author and Finisher of our faith. He gives you all the faith you need today. It does not help you to look at the petrol in your tank. Invisible, a source of power, ready for use, the petrol is in the tank. And so it is with faith. It is given to you, not to admire, but to experience its working.

Faith works, to protect us against the fiery arrows of the enemy.

The Shield of Faith

The enemy shoots his fiery arrows out of invisible unexpected positions. Therefore, this shield is so important. David said: "The Lord is my shield" (Psa. 28:7).

God said to Abraham: "I am thy shield, and thy exceeding great reward" (Gen. 15:1).

Not only is faith our shield; the Lord Himself is our shield also. A soldier who handles a shield does not put it behind him, but in front of him. Then he is covered. That is the right position. When the Lord is our shield, He must go before us, and we must remain behind Him. Many are willing to work for the Lord, but they walk in front of Him, and thus the fiery arrows of the evil one can reach them without difficulty.

No, the Lord says: "Follow Me!" He will go before us. Our position demands that we work only on His instructions and go where He calls us. Sometimes we have to wait until the Lord tells it to us very clearly. If we work out of our own enthusiasm, we can expect defeat. Even a small service must be inspired by the Lord. Our prayer should be: "Lord, what do You want me to do? Where must I go?" We can then remain in the centre of the will of God, and there it is safe. If the direction is not yet quite clear, we must wait on the Lord, and this waiting can be a blessing. When we follow Him, we live in the attitude of faith. It is this attitude of faith that keeps us close to the Lord, to Him who gives us the power of faith. When the enthusiasm comes from ourselves, we can be very active, but without instruction from the Master we go unprotected in front of Him, so that the fiery arrows of the devil can do their horrible work unhindered.

When the Lord tells us: "Do this!", He also gives us the faith to do it, and that is why we can obey. Then we will not be ashamed and miracles will happen in our lives. Then we do not work in our own strength, but in the strength we receive from the Lord.

"It is His business, His honour, the cause for which we stand."

Do not begin a work when you are not quite sure that the Lord has instructed you to do it. When fellow-Christians tell you that they have had guidance for you, then you may quietly say: "As long as the Lord has not said it to me personally, I will not do it." Paul is an example for us in this matter. He always let the Holy Spirit guide him. If the Holy Spirit said to him: "Do not go there," then he did not go. He really longed to go to all these heathen places in Asia Minor, but the Spirit did not let him do it (Acts 16:6). But once he received a very clear revelation from the Lord that he had to go to Macedonia, he obeyed, and the result was great blessing and miracles. Paul had the true missionary method: obedience.

With the instruction, the Lord gives grace, strength, faith and courage to carry out the instructed task.

"Where the Lord guides, He provides."

Likewise, when the Holy Spirit gives us special gifts, we may not use these riches according to our own discretion. Again and again, we must look up in faith unto Jesus and say: "Lord, only behind You!" If at this moment the Lord tells you to lay hands on a blind person, then you may not say: "Yes, Lord, but I do not have the gift of healing." When the Lord calls us, then He gives also the courage of faith and everything that we need to carry out the task. When He sends us, then He gives the strength and the grace to obey. The point is to have the right attitude of faith. In the beginning it may be difficult, but by faith we receive strength to reach our goal. If we should have to work up this faith ourselves, then the whole enterprise would become rather doubtful. Today we may be very strong in faith, and tomorrow this may not be so. Today we may feel fine and healthy, tomorrow we may feel ill and weak. So it is with everything that we have from ourselves. Today we may feel like being able to remove mountains, tomorrow we may be without any courage. But when the Lord gives us His faith, it is "eternity faith" that never wavers. It is grounded on God's Word. All these things we must exercise and learn.

"Acquaint now thyself with him, and be at peace" (Job 22:21).

A missionary who worked in a dangerous place was

once asked: "Are you never afraid?" His answer was: "Yes, sometimes I am, but the rock on which I stand never shakes." He knew that he worked on the instructions of his Master and that was sufficient. His starting-point was not his own faith and strength, but the courage of faith that he received from God.

In Gal. 2:20 Paul says: "Yet not I, but Christ liveth in me; and the life which I now live in the flesh I live by the faith of the Son of God, who loved me, and gave himself for me." Not his own faith, but Jesus' faith was his life.

Even those among us who have a strong faith can waver. For instance, look at the disciples. Often Jesus had to say to them: "You of little faith!" How was it with Peter when he was empowered by the Lord to walk on the water? When he saw the waves he doubted, and began to sink. As long as we look unto Jesus, He gives us faith. That is why a soldier must always remain behind the shield of faith. So he gets the vision from a safe hiding-place. Then the impossible becomes possible.

16. JOY

"The joy of the Lord is your strength" (Neh. 8:10).

It is so important to know that in the final battle the joy of the Holy Spirit is available for us in all circumstances.

Once a prisoner wrote me a letter. "It is Christmas Eve. I am alone in my cell. There are no Christmas presents for me on the table. There is nothing that reminds me of Christmas. On the empty walls there are no Christmas decorations. But in my heart is Christmas joy, because Jesus lives there, and that is the greatest joy a human being can have. I could not send Corrie ten

Boom a present, but I went on my knees and prayed for you for two hours. That was my Christmas present for you and it made my own heart still more joyful."

I remember a dark day in Ravensbruck. Betsie and I talked much with the Lord. Horrible things happened around us. There were days that we said to each other: "More terrible than today it can never be." But the next day was still more terrible. Despair was on all faces, for there was no salt in any of the meals that day. When you are slowly starving, salt is very important. Several women died that day, one of them as a result of a cruel beating. The electric light had failed, and after sunset we were in the deepest darkness. I put my arm around Betsie. She spoke about heaven and told me that shortly before we were arrested she had read about heaven in a booklet by the Sadhu Sundar Singh. We had a talk with the Lord. He spoke and we listened; then He listened while we spoke. Then we went to sleep under the dirty coat which we used as a blanket, and Betsie said: "What a wonderful day we have had. The Lord has shown us so much of Himself."

Joy in a Prison in Africa

When it rains in tropical countries, then it really pours. I visited a prison in Ruanda. It was only a small building, but many prisoners were sitting outside on the ground.

"Where do you sleep at night?" I asked.

"Half of us sleep inside, the others must stay outside, because there are too many prisoners." Some had a banana leaf, others had a branch or an old newspaper to sit on. The uniforms were grey, and the faces of the Negroes were dark and angry. It was all so sad. Could I bring *here* the gospel, the tidings of great joy? No, I could not, but the Holy Spirit could. I prayed: "Lord, the fruit of the Spirit is joy. Give me an ocean of joy to share with these poor fellows." He did what I asked. I could almost shout for joy. I told them of a Friend whose name is Jesus, who is good and so full of love, who never leaves us alone, who is strong and has the answer for all the great problems of sin and death. I said: "Perhaps you think, 'That is not for us, our lives are too terrible.' But fellows, I was in a prison where it was worse than here, where ninety-five thousand women were killed or died, including my own sister. There I experienced that Jesus is always with me. He lives in my heart; He has never left me alone." I felt in my heart a great joy that imparted itself to the men who were sitting in the pouring rain. Then I saw that the joy of the Holy Spirit can be experienced in all circumstances. "This Friend and Saviour, Jesus, will live in your hearts. Who will open the door of his heart to Him?" They all, including the guards, put up their hands, and their faces beamed.

Jesus came as a light into the world, so that everyone who believes on Him should not abide in darkness (John 12:46).

When I said goodbye, all the prisoners accompanied me to the car. The guards did not seem to be afraid that someone would run away. They came with us, and stood around the car.

"What do they say?" I asked my interpreter. She laughed and said: "Old woman, come back, come back, and tell us more about Jesus."

My interpreter, a missionary, said: "I have been here once, but thought it was so hopeless that I stopped my visits. Now I have seen what the Holy Spirit can do. I will come here every week." She has done so, and the feast is going on!

4

LIFE IN THE END-TIME

17. SIGNS OF THE TIMES

"Watch therefore, for ye know neither the day nor the hour" (Matt. 25:13).

WE LIVE NOW IN THOSE DAYS of which Jesus spoke. People are ready to know all about the weather conditions (e.g. when the sun goes down red, it will be nice weather the next day), but what about the signs of the times?

"Ye hypocrites, ye can discern the face of the sky and of the earth; but how is it that ye do not discern this time?" Jesus says (Luke 12:56).

The end-time has started already. Those who pay attention to the signs of the times will not doubt this at all. If we watch the events in the Middle East, in Israel and the Arab States, then we cannot do anything else but look expectantly for the coming of the Lord. Every day, every hour brings us nearer to His coming. We see many more signs of the times than ever before. We can see them in the newspapers. It is a command of the Lord that we must mind the signs of the times. I believe everything that is written in the Bible about the coming again of Jesus. Everything that was written about the first coming of Jesus happened exactly as foretold, so

69

that which is written about His coming again will happen likewise.

This does not mean that I understand everything, but that is not necessary. For instance, in Ezek. 38 is written that there will be a mighty army coming on horseback. These days soldiers do not go on horseback; they use tanks and aeroplanes! But now I read in a newspaper that Russia has bought seventy per cent of all the horses of the world for its army. What I do not understand of the Bible, I do not throw away, but hang it on a hook, as it were. Later I read or hear more about it, and then, when I understand it, it is added to my knowledge of God's Word, and I just take it off the hook. So it is with Ezek. 38. What Jesus Himself said in Matt. 24 and in Luke 21 is happening in our days: wars, rumours of wars, one nation against the other, earthquakes, famines, persecution. All this is happening in a far greater measure than ever before.

The clearest sign is Israel, which has returned to its own land. It has, with its six million people, beaten off the threat of a superior force of forty-five million people in the six-day war in June 1967. Many who were concerned about the "apple of God's eye" saw the baffling reality of a swift victory for Israel as a very clear sign of the times.

We do not know the day, neither the hour, in which Jesus will come again. But neither do we know a day nor an hour in which He could not come. The whole world lives now in this expectation; something must happen by which the great problems will be solved. When we look at world history in the light of the Bible, we can find many clear signs: Luke 21:26 (R.S.V.): "Men fainting with fear and with foreboding of what is coming on the world." Everywhere in the world are people who are in great fear of an atomic war, and they are rightly afraid. There will be earthquakes, epidemics and famines. "And because iniquity shall abound, the love of many shall wax cold" (Matt. 24:12).

"Many shall run to and fro, and knowledge shall be increased" (Dan. 12:4). Just look at the development of space-travel!

Mother Basilea Schlink says in her book *The End is Coming*, "It may be true that this end-time has started, so that on the one side many things begin to be outlined on a larger scale, while on the other hand certain things about which we have been in the dark until now, become more clear, though on a smaller scale. Nevertheless, this does not alter the fact that very many details are still secret to us, and we have to wait for the hour that they will be brought to light."

The only thing we have to do is what the Holy Scriptures teach us. We need to raise our voices like the voice of a trumpet so that as many people as possible will awake—first of all those who belong to the Church of Christ. We have to proclaim loudly that the end is near, so that people will be startled out of their everyday rest and security by this godly message, as through the roaring of the lion (Amos 3:8); that they will fear and get ready to meet their God. We urgently need such a "blowing of the trumpet", since the day of the Lord draws near, as the prophet Joel says: "Blow the trumpet in Zion, sanctify a fast, call a solemn assembly" (Joel 2:15). For we need to prepare ourselves for all that soon will come to pass.

When we think of the last great battle, we must realise that not only is the future at stake, but that in this present time we are engaged in a warfare. Already we are standing in the midst of the battle. If we have our eyes and ears open, we see how the enemy is marching on from all sides. We do not have to battle against flesh and blood, but against the rulers of the darkness of this world (Eph. 6:12).

The armour is not only necessary for the battle which we have to fight in the future, but also for this time. The devil is a refined psychologist. He has been studying in practice for over six thousand years how to seduce men. He knows our weak spots. He is just like a good cattle-dealer who has to go around a cow only once to see all its weak spots. The devil is not omnipresent, but he has an exceptionally good active secret service at his disposal in his army of demons.

But: praise the Lord! "they that be with us are more than they that be with them" (2 Kings 6:16). The Syrian army that the servant of Elisha saw was a terrible, forbidding reality, but when his eyes were opened, he saw something far more important; the angels, a heavenly host with horses and chariots of fire, that had come to protect Elisha. And when we look at this invisible reality, then we know that we stand on victory ground.

In the concentration camp, where I was so often confronted with death, the Lord often gave me grace to see the whole situation more or less in the light of eternity, and then everything was so simple, so uncomplicated. It was as if I saw myself; I stood there, and there stood the devil. The devil was much, much stronger than I, but Jesus stood at my side, and He is far stronger than the devil. And because I stood at Jesus' side, I was more than conqueror. That is reality.

It is essential that we realise in these days that Jesus is Conqueror! To stand at His side, to follow Him, to be hidden with Him in God; that is the safe position for every soldier of Jesus in this time and in the coming final battle.

18. GUIDANCE

"Don't let the world around you squeeze you into its own mould, but let God remould your minds from within, so that you may prove in practice that the plan of God for you is good, meets all his demands and moves towards the goal of true maturity" (Rom. 12:2, Phillips).

A soldier has to know his marching orders. He must know where he has to go and especially it is so important at this time that we see the leading of the Lord very clearly. People often ask me: "How can I know the will of God? How does the Lord lead His children?"

We often make the words "surrender" and "leading" too complicated. When we discover what causes our view to be so dim, the meaning of these words becomes clear. There can be a fog around us, caused by the temptations of the enemy, but it is also possible that the "window" has become dirty on the inside by our sins. It can also happen that God puts His hand on the window, but especially then He is very close to us. We must get accustomed, and train ourselves, to be guided by God.

The Holy Spirit makes us sensitive to His guidance. Often we must wait quietly, but waiting on the Lord can be a blessing in itself. We must learn to make our decisions in the presence of the Lord, when we are conscious of His nearness. Often God leads through the Bible, therefore we must know the Bible well. The better we know the Bible, the more His Word gives light on our path. The Lord also leads us by our feelings. However, when we rely too much on our feelings, we can become too subjective, but it is not necessary that the leading of the Lord has nothing to do with our feelings. Just imagine someone telling you: "I have been married now for six months, but for some weeks I have not felt that I am married." Then there is something wrong with that marriage.

God also uses our feelings to control our relationships with Himself. The fruit of the Spirit is peace and joy, and that does not go without our feelings. Harmony with God goes together with harmony with Spirit-filled believers. Also in this we can find guidance. When God calls us His children, will He then not guide us safely as our Father?

"All who follow the leading of God's Spirit are God's own sons" (Rom. 8:14, Phillips).

These things we cannot understand with our logical thinking. We must not forget that all leading of God belongs to the "foolishness of God", which is the highest wisdom, and can only be understood by faith. "We do, of course, speak 'wisdom' among those who are spiritually mature, but it is not what is called wisdom by this world, not by the powers-that-be, who soon will be only the powers that have been. The wisdom we speak of is that mysterious secret wisdom of God which He planned before the creation of our glory today" (1 Cor. 2:6,7, Phillips).

God wants to take the lead in our lives. He longs for hidden fellowship with His children. In the Bible we read that this fellowship was broken through the Fall, but that it is restored again through Jesus Christ. He wants to teach us so that we get to know Him better. He will conform us to His image, and will reach other people through us. But we can only bring His light to others when we are set apart for Him, sanctified. Sanctification means that God separates in our hearts light from darkness. The Holy Spirit brings us nearer to God and makes us conformable to Christ. He convicts us of sin, but He is also the Comforter and He shows us Jesus. Then the separation between light and darkness comes into being. The devil accuses us to discourage us. Every feeling of guilt in our hearts we must confess immediately to the Lord, so that the vision gets clear again. "If the Son therefore shall make you free, ye shall be free indeed" (John 8:36).

The Holy Spirit makes the Bible a love-letter from God to His children. When we do not read the Bible often we get confused ideas about God. It is good to pray first before reading the Bible: "Lord, show me my sins." For the Word of God says: "Your sins have hid His face from you" (Isa. 59:2b). When we confess our sins, the Lord forgives and His blood cleanses us (1 John 1:7,9).

It is not sufficient to pray: "Lord, help me not to sin." We must humble ourselves, confess our sins and ask forgiveness. Then He forgives. Let this be our prayer: "Lord, give me today a clear vision of Your leading through the reading of the Bible. Help me also to tell others about what I read in Your Word." Then you will experience that what you read can help you, and also others through you.

The devil does his utmost to turn our eyes away from Jesus. He tries to get us so far away that we explain everything by our intellect and argue God's Word. We must never forget that the Bible belongs to the plane of God's foolishness. We can never bring the things of foolishness of God down to the lower level of human wisdom, without losing a blessing. But through the Holy Spirit we can bring the wisdom of the wise up to the higher plane of the foolishness of God. His Spirit will use our limited language to reveal to us His divine ordinances, His commandments and the knowledge of His being. Then we take our position in God's strategy: we have the outlook from a safe, hidden place.

The foolishness of God can only be understood by faith: the wisdom of men through our senses and intellect. The Bible gives us many clear promises that the Lord leads us and always will lead us: "I will instruct thee and teach thee in the way which thou shalt go: I will guide thee with mine eye" (Psa. 32:8). "And thine ears shall hear a word behind thee, saying, This is the way, walk ye in it, when ye turn to the right hand, and when ye turn to the left" (Isa. 30:21). "And the Lord shall guide thee continually, and satisfy thy soul" (Isa. 58:11).

The Lord leads us through His Word, through feelings and through circumstances, and mostly through all three together. It is such a wonderful experience when the Lord speaks through our feelings and our thinking when we pray and listen to the Lord. The prayer becomes then a conversation from both sides. We on our side must also learn to expect that the Lord acts according to His promises and leads us on His way.

> "Obey my voice, and I will be your God, and ye shall be my people: and walk ye in all the ways that I have commanded you, that it may be well unto you" (Jer. 7:23).

The Lord is really a good Shepherd, and a good Shepherd leads His sheep. Nevertheless again and again I hear Christians say that they do not get any guidance. When we do not know the will of the Lord, the cause is often doubt and disobedience.

After my time in the concentration camp all the cruelties of the Gestapo left such an impression on me, and I was so confused, that I said to my friends: "I will work anywhere in the whole world, wherever the Lord sends me, but there is one country where I hope He will never send me, and that is Germany. I never want to hear one word of German again."

That was disobedience. Obedience says: "Yes, Father." Disobedience says: "Yes, but . . ."

I went to America and there came a shadow over my prayer life. When I asked God for guidance, I did not get any answer. Then I said: "Lord, why is this? I know that you are my good Shepherd, so I must be the cause. Have I been disobedient in any way?" Then the Lord said very clearly: "Germany." "Then I will go to Germany too, Lord."

As soon as I was willing for this, the light came back to my prayer life. I knew again where the Lord wanted to send me. I received from my good Shepherd direct guidance in the little things of daily life and also for my future plans. You must understand that a "tramp for the Lord", as I am, not only needs guidance for one day, but often for many months ahead, to be able to prepare the working programme. I went to Germany later on. After all, the Germans are not my enemies; my best friends live in Germany. But I also found there the enemies who had been so cruel to my sister Betsie and me. But then I have learnt a very valuable lesson that when Jesus tells us that we have to love our enemies, He also gives us all the love that He demands from us. In the centre of the will of God is rest. Our times are in God's hands: all our wheres, whens, whys and hows. Although we do not underestimate the power and the urge for destruction of the devil, we have nothing to fear, for we are under the protection of the Victor over all powers of darkness. We experience that we are with Jesus hidden in God. There is nothing better than that. Just as there is quietness and peace in the centre of a hurricane, so there is also quietness and peace in the centre of the will of God. Yes, with Jesus hidden in God—there is quietness and peace. Then there can be a storm around us, but one is safe.

I have experienced that in America. There was a terrible hurricane, and a thundering roar. Suddenly it was quiet, absolutely quiet. Nothing moved. I asked what had happened. I was told: "Now we are in the centre of the hurricane. There is quietness and rest."

So it is when one totally surrenders to the strong hands of Jesus. Then one need not be afraid, even "Though the earth be removed, and though the mountains be carried into the midst of the sea" (Psa. 46:2).

God Does Perform Miracles

On my trip to the Far East, I was once in Formosa. The Lord told me very clearly that I had to work in several countries and that I therefore should buy an air ticket. But I had no money. The Lord is not only my Shepherd, He is also my Treasurer and He is very wealthy. Sometimes He tries my faith, but when I am obedient then the money comes just in time. "The cattle upon a thousand hills" belong to Him (Psa. 50:10). Sometimes, when I need money, I say: "Father, I believe that you must sell a cow from the cattle on one of your mountains." And then He answers my prayer.

When I went to the travel agency and said to the girl at the desk: "Will you write down the names of the places for which I need an air ticket? First to Hong Kong, then to Sydney in Australia, Auckland in New Zealand, back again to Sydney, then to Cape Town in South Africa, Tel Aviv in Israel and then to Amsterdam in Holland." She wrote it down and then asked: "What is your end destination?" "Heaven." "How do you write that?" I spelt "H-E-A-V-E-N." When she had written it down, she understood what I had said and answered: "Oh, but I do not mean that."

"But I meant it, but you do not need to write it down, because I have already got my ticket."

"How did you receive it?"

"About two thousand years ago there was One who bought my ticket for heaven and I had only to accept it from Him. That was Jesus when at the Cross He carried my sins and so made the way to heaven free for me."

A Chinese clerk, who also worked in the agency and had listened to our conversation, passed by. He said: "Yes, that is true." I asked him: "Have you a reservation in heaven?"

"Yes, I have. I have received Jesus as my Saviour and Lord and He has made me a child of God. And a child of God has a place in heaven in the house of the Father." I said to him: "Brother, will you see to it that this girl will not be too late with her reservation for a place in heaven?"

Then I turned to the girl: "When you do not have a reservation for a seat in a plane, you get into great difficulties, but when you do not have a place in heaven, you will end up in far greater difficulties."

"Brother, you must take care that she is not too late."

Was that a joke? No, I meant it and I mean it also for you who are reading this. Have you made your reservation for a place in heaven? If you are not certain of your salvation, then make a decision now. "As many as received him (Jesus), to them gave he power to become the sons of God" (John 1:12).

When the ticket for the journey was ready, the Lord had given me exactly all the money I needed. Thankfully I looked in the booklet with all the different tickets. Sydney—Auckland—Sydney. But then I saw that not Cape Town followed, but Tel Aviv. And then the tickets were written out for Tel Aviv—Cape Town—Amsterdam. I phoned the travel agency and asked the girl: "Why have you changed my schedule? My Chief has told me that I must go first to Cape Town and after that to Tel Aviv. Now you have changed the sequence, first Tel Aviv and after that Cape Town. God is my Master and I must obey Him."

"But that is impossible," the girl said. "There is not a direct airline from Australia to Africa. There is no island in the Indian Ocean for the plane to land to be refuelled. That is why you must first go to Tel Aviv."

"No, I must do what my Chief has told me. Perhaps I must pray for an island in the Indian Ocean. But my schedule has to remain as He had told me."

An hour later the girl phoned: "Did you really pray for an island in the Indian Ocean? I just received a telegram from Qantas, the Australian airline. They have begun to use the Cocos Islands, and now there is a direct route from Australia to Africa, via the Cocos Islands and Mauritius."

"Now you see, Miss, that God does not make mistakes in His plans!"

There is nothing too great for God's power, and nothing too small for His love.

19. SANCTIFICATION

"He that is unjust, let him be unjust still: and he which is filthy, let him be filthy still: and he that is righteous, let him be righteous still: and he that is holy, let him be holy still" (Rev. 22:11).

These days more than ever before, it is one or the other. The command "Let him be righteous still" is the training, the battle and the victory in reality, all at the same time and all in view of the coming end-time. Our little "decent" sins are victories for the enemy. That is why we ought to walk very carefully. In this time of preparation or perhaps we can speak of a breathing-space—the longing to get the prophetical armour must be the most serious prayer for the Church of believers. What we need for the battle is to be ready and armed. Therefore: Be filled with the Spirit! Fight and bring

forth fruit! I cannot help but think of the Israelites who
kept their weapons with them when they worked in the
fields.

"The fruit of the Spirit is love, joy, peace, longsuffering, gentleness, goodness, faith, meekness, temperance" (Gal. 5:22,23).

What an armour! There is not written "fruits", but
"fruit". Not like an apple, a pear and a banana, but like
several grapes in a bunch. It all belongs together.

He who is filled with the Holy Spirit goes relaxed
through life, for he knows that it is not a matter of
trying but of trusting, and yielding to Him, "Who shall
also confirm you unto the end, that ye may be blameless
in the day of our Lord Jesus Christ" (1 Cor. 1:8).

It is the Lord Jesus Christ Himself who by His Spirit
makes us live sanctified lives. He makes us obedient to
what the Bible says:

"But whatever happens, make sure your everyday
life is worthy of the gospel of Christ. So that whether
I do come and see you, or merely hear about you from
a distance, I may know that you are standing fast in
a united spirit, battling with a single mind for the
faith of the gospel and not caring two straws for your
enemies" (Phil. 1:27, 28, Phillips).

Jesus is Victor! He has conquered Satan, the power of
sin and the world. He that is in you, in me, is Victor!
We cannot overcome the enemy. We are powerless in
ourselves. We are crucified with Christ, but also resurrected with Him unto a new life, here and now. It is the
Lord Himself who accomplishes this. When we know
this, we can see God's way, even when we have to go the
hard way.

"We know that all things work together for good to them that love God" (Rom. 8:28).

It is by the grace of God that we can be conquerors. To be a conqueror, one must allow God to live His life in and through us. Again and again He has to break us; that is to say, He breaks the things in us that protect and maintain "self". We must surrender totally to Him, and let Him do all that is necessary. Thus He gets more and more room in us. He does not want only a part of us, but to fill our whole heart with His power; to fill us more and more with Himself. That means a closer fellowship with Him. That is glory!

The promises in the Book of Revelation are for all overcomers, from the beginning until the end.

"And He said unto me, It is done. I am Alpha and Omega, the beginning and the end. I will give unto him that is athirst of the fountain of the water of life freely. He that overcometh shall inherit all things; and I will be his God, and he shall be my son" (Rev. 21:6,7).

When we are totally emptied of ourselves, we can be full of the Holy Spirit. Then we are conquerors, and are able to accept all things from His hand. Besides this, we are being prepared to inherit all things. "And every man that hath this hope in him purifieth himself, even as He is pure" (1 John 3:3). The contrasts between the Holy Spirit and self become more and more acute. But the Bible has a mighty answer: It is possible to be cleansed. No trying, no striving, but trusting in Him, looking unto Him in His Word, in our prayers, in our fellowship with Him. Then he cleanses us through His Word, that we bring forth more fruit as a branch on the vine. Jesus said: "I am the true vine, and my Father is the husbandman. Every branch in me that beareth not fruit he taketh away: and every branch that beareth fruit, he purgeth it, that it may bring forth more fruit" (John 15:1,2). We cannot direct the knife with which He is going to purge us. It is to no purpose when we ourselves cut off a bit here and purge some there. The knife is in His hand, in the hand of the husbandman. He will cleanse and sanctify us.

"The fruit of the Spirit is love, joy, peace, longsuffering, gentleness, goodness, faith, meekness, temperance: against such there is no law. And they that are Christ's have crucified the flesh with the affections and lusts. If we live in the Spirit, let us also walk in the Spirit. Let us not be desirous of vain glory, provoking one another, envying one another" (Gal. 5:22–26).

Sanctification is: Be filled with the Holy Spirit!

20. MARTYRDOM

"But rejoice, inasmuch as ye are partakers of Christ's sufferings: that, when his glory shall be revealed, ye may be glad also with exceeding joy" (1 Pet. 4:13).

Peter, who himself died as a martyr, tells us in his letters what it means to be one. Perhaps there have never been so many children of God who died as martyrs as in our day. Probably many more will follow. That is said quite clearly in the Book of Revelation.

I remember as a child saying to my father: "I am afraid that I will never be strong enough to die as a martyr."

But he said: "When you have to go on a journey, when do I give you the money for the fare—two weeks before?"

"No, Daddy, on the day that I am leaving."

"Precisely, and that is what the Saviour does also."

He does not give us grace now for something we may have to pass through later on. If He thinks we are worthy to die as a martyr, He gives us the strength for it at that moment. Once I was in Burundi. A civil war had broken out there. Every day people were imprisoned, including Christians. At night we heard shooting when many were killed. The children of God were in uncertainty. What would the future bring? On Sunday morning I spoke in a church. One could really feel the tension. Who would be arrested this week and killed? Who would be still alive next Sunday?

Then I spoke on 2 Cor. 4:17, "For our light affliction, which is but for a moment, worketh for us a far more exceeding and eternal weight of glory." I told them of an experience I had gone through myself. It has been recorded in my book *A Prisoner and Yet* ...

When I was in a concentration camp during the war—Ravensbruck—the Bible was called there "das Lugenbuch" (The Book of Lies). It was a miracle that I still had my Bible. The room in which we lived with seven hundred women was so dirty that we were all full of lice. The guards and the other officers would never enter our room, because they were afraid to get vermin from us. God can use even lice, for that is why I could bring a message from God's Word twice a day.

One day we got a new supervisor whose name was Lony. She was a fellow-prisoner, a cruel woman; she told the guards everything we did. One day I opened my Bible. A friend of mine said: "Don't do it today. Lony is sitting behind you. If she knows that you have a Bible, she will see to it that you will be killed in a cruel way."

I prayed: "God, give me the strength even now to bring Your Word." He answered that prayer. I read the Bible, brought the message, prayed and then we sang a hymn: "Commit thy ways unto the Lord." When the song had finished, we heard someone call: "Another song like that!" It was Lony; she had enjoyed the singing. Afterwards I got a chance to explain the gospel to her, to show her the way of salvation. I am not a hero. When you know that what you are saying can mean a cruel death, then every word is as heavy as lead. But I have never had such a joy and peace in my heart as when I gave that message, neither before that time, nor afterwards.

God gave me grace to be a martyr. Now I know from experience that, when God demands it of us, when He thinks we are worthy to be martyrs, He will also give us grace. When I told the church this story, a great joy came into the hearts of these people. Perhaps I must say it was a sad joy. Everyone knew it could be the last time that they were assembled. But I felt as one does when one is at the death-bed of a child of God. Suddenly one sees the things of this world from God's point of view, the light of eternity. It gives a feeling of a certain freedom. One sees the great things great, the small things small. The things that are important in everyday life suddenly become very unimportant.

When a child of God is entering into the presence of the Lord, then one does not ask: "What's the time? When do we have dinner? How much money do we have in hand? What kind of dress shall I wear?" No, all these things fall away; they are no longer important. What, then, is important? The important things are the texts of God's Word, especially those that speak of heaven; for instance, where Jesus says: "In my Father's house are many mansions: if it were not so, I would have told you" (John 14:2).

Important is what is written about the glory of heaven: "O death, where is thy sting?" (1 Cor. 15:55). I thank my God for the victory through Jesus Christ! "While we look not at the things which are seen, but at the things which are not seen: for the things which are seen are temporal; but the things which are not seen are eternal" (2 Cor. 4:18).

I could also tell them that, when we are found worthy to die as martyrs, martyrs' crowns are awaiting us. Eternity is long, but time is short. In that same week, many members of that church were arrested and martyred.

It is necessary, when we prepare ourselves for the end-time, also to be prepared to die for Jesus.

A missionary went back to China. It was still possible then, but very dangerous. Someone asked her: "Are you not afraid to go back?" She said: "There is but one thing I am afraid of, that I would not be willing to be like the grain of wheat that has to die in the ground." Did not Jesus say that following Him means to lose our lives for Him? And that is really to find our lives.

What does the Word of God say about martyrdom?

"Beloved, think it not strange concerning the fiery trial which is to try you, as though some strange thing happened unto you: but rejoice, inasmuch as ye are partakers of Christ's sufferings; that, when His glory shall be revealed, ye may be glad also with exceeding joy" (1 Pet. 4:12,13).

"Only let your conversation be as it becometh the gospel of Christ: that whether I come and see you, or else be absent, I may hear of your affairs, that ye stand fast in one spirit ... For unto you it is given in the behalf of Christ, not only to believe on him, but also to suffer for his sake; having the same conflict

which ye saw in me, and now hear to be in me" (Phil.
1:27,29,30).

"And they overcame him by the blood of the Lamb,
and by the word of their testimony; and they loved
not their lives unto the death" (Rev. 12:11).

Yes, the finished work at the Cross of Calvary, the
power of the blood of Jesus, is our great victory. We can
take this into account in our battle, now and in the future. But the word of our testimony also is a power to
gain the victory. We must always be ready to confess
the gospel of Jesus Christ before devil and people. If we
don't do it, then there is something wrong. When we are
ready to confess, then we are also ready to suffer. How is
it with you? Are you ready to tell everyone who is
willing to listen? It is settled for all eternity that Jesus is
Victor; that the whole world belongs to Him!

Also, we must not love our lives unto the death. In
Kampala there is a cross by the wayside, where once the
"martyrs of Kampala" passed by. They were young men,
almost children, who served a very wicked king about a
hundred years ago. He was a homosexual, and wanted
to use them. But these boys were Christians and did not
want this. Then they were warned: "You will be burned
alive." In spite of this threat they did not want to be
guilty of such a sin. So they were all chained together
and had to walk a long way to the place where they
would be burned alive. As they walked they sang hymns.
They knew: now we must die, because we are faithful to
Jesus and His commandments. The Lord gave them
grace and joy! When the chains got mixed up and they
almost fell over each other, they laughed joyfully. Then
one after the other was burned alive, and when one had
his turn, the others who were waiting for the same cruel
death encouraged him: "Only a few minutes and then
you are with the Lord. We are allowed to do this be-

cause we follow Him who carried His Cross for us. It is an honour to die as a martyr." They could even sing. Thus the Lord was honoured by these awful events. Those fifteen-year-old boys did not love their lives unto the death. The Lord gave them grace for it. He will also give us grace should we be counted worthy to suffer martyrdom.

By His resurrection power the Lord gives us now, and even more so in the end-time, all we need to be strong in Him. "Now I long to know Christ and the power shown by his resurrection: now I long to share his sufferings, even to die as he died, so that I may perhaps attain as he did, the resurrection from the dead" (Phil. 3:10, Phillips).

When we die with Jesus, then we also may be resurrected with Him into a new life. By this I do not only mean the resurrection to life after death, but to experience His resurrection power so that "being made conformable unto his death" can be a reality even now.

In *A Prisoner and Yet* ... I tell what I once experienced in Ravensbruck. We had to stand for "Naked roll-call". I never felt so miserable and so ashamed. They took away all our clothing and so we had to stand in the icy cold. I said to my sister Betsie: "This is the very worst thing the enemy has ever done to us. I can hardly bear it." Suddenly I saw Jesus on the Cross. The Bible says: "They parted His garments among them." Then I understood through my own experience a little bit of His suffering: He hung naked on the Cross for me! When I realised this I understood a little of the ocean of love which Jesus has for us that He carried such a punishment for our sins. That made me so thankful that I was more able to bear my own suffering. When we die with Him, then He also gives us the resurrection power and all the grace we need to live for Him.

"But they that wait upon the Lord shall renew their strength" (Isa. 40:31).

God never lets the dominion go out of His hands. When we are in the midst of the battle, sometimes it seems to be one great chaos. Then suddenly the Lord shows us: "I am still here!"

I have experienced this in Africa at a time when the devil had broken loose and so many terrible things were happening. In the newspapers one could read of all sorts of cruelty, but when I listened to what the children of God had to say, I was glad to hear that God had never left His children in Africa alone and that the devil could not go any further than God allowed. We do not always understand this, but some day we shall.

A troop of rebels in the Congo came into a village. The leader asked: "What is that house?" "That is the house of God." He took a stone to throw into it, but at that same moment he was killed by a bullet. The bullet must have been misfired by one of his own people. In another village the rebels decided to kill all the Christians. They had come together in a hut to discuss this inhuman plan. At that moment lightning struck the hut and all were killed.

When the rebels advanced on a school where two hundred children of missionaries lived, they planned to kill both children and teachers. In the school they knew of the danger and therefore went to prayer. Their only protection was a fence and a couple of soldiers, while the enemy, who came closer and closer, amounted to several hundreds. When the rebels were close by, suddenly something happened: they turned around and ran away! The next day the same thing happened and again on the third day. One of the rebels was wounded and was brought to the mission hospital. When the doctor was busy dressing his wounds, he asked him: "Why did you not break into the school as you planned?" "We could not do it. We saw hundreds of soldiers in white uniforms and we became scared." In Africa soldiers never wear white uniforms, so it must have been angels. What a wonderful thing that the Lord can open the eyes of the enemy so that they see angels! We, as children of God, do not need to see them with our human eyes. We have the Bible and faith, and by faith we see invisible things.

In Havana, Cuba, I was once a guest in a boarding-school for girls. There were children from two to seventeen years. "May I tell the girls something?" I asked after dinner. "No, they still have to do all their home-work for tomorrow. You may speak for five minutes, no longer!" After four minutes the lights suddenly went out. "Please will you continue until the lights go on again? The children cannot work in the dark!" I told about all sorts of adventures, my journeys, meetings with children, happy and sad stories. So I was able to tell about the Lord Jesus, who He was and what He is to us in our want and joy. He had said: "Lo, I am with you alway, even unto the end of the world" (Matt. 28:20). After an hour the lights came on again. The children started their home-work. A little girl came to me, put her arms around my neck, and whispered: "I believe that Jesus broke the lights so that you could tell us about Him." In days to come we shall often have to fix our eyes upon the Lord. Often it will seem a lost cause. Often Jesus will have to break the lights, so that we can listen to Him.

In Hong Kong there was a terrible situation among the refugees. So many people came over the border that there was simply no room left. Although the authorities very much regretted this, the frontier had to be closed. Once a day policemen searched the no-man's-land, where the refugees tried to find a hiding-place in the mountains and hills. The rest of the day they could move around freely. Now, some missionaries had found out that there was lack of food among these people. They took baskets of bread and drinks and went out to the refugees when the police were not there. They did not only give them food, but also the Bread of Life. Many of these people accepted the Lord Jesus as their Saviour. They received a Bible and a Bible correspondence course. Later many of them were found by the police and sent back to Red China. But also many became real missionaries there. In Hong Kong many letters were received for the Bible correspondence course. So these people were used to bring the gospel to a country where it is impossible for Christians to meet together. So many were in despair, but the angels have rejoiced about what happened. God never makes a mistake! Often we shall have to fix our eyes upon Jesus to see that God has no problems; only plans. There is never a panic in heaven.

21. JESUS IS VICTOR

"Because thou hast kept the word of my patience, I also will keep thee from the hour of temptation, which shall come upon all the world, to try them that dwell upon the earth. Behold, I come quickly: hold that fast which thou hast, that no man take thy crown" (Rev. 3:10,11).

The Lord Jesus demands much of us. He said: "For I say unto you, That except your righteousness shall exceed the righteousness of the scribes and Pharisees, ye shall in no case enter into the kingdom of heaven" (Matt. 5:20).

Nowadays people are inclined to belittle God. It is as if they look through the wrong end of a telescope. Their knowledge seems to be unlimited. God is far away and small; for many no longer to be seen. The possibilities for man are indeed unlimited, but only when he does not limit the promises of God through his unbelief. As the mountains and the stars of heaven are unshakable, so the works of Jesus are standing firm as a rock, and even more so, because they bear the stamp of eternity.

"Fear not: for I have redeemed thee, I have called thee by thy name; thou art mine. When thou passest through the waters, I will be with thee; and through the rivers, they shall not overflow thee: when thou walkest through the fire, thou shalt not be burned; neither shall the flame kindle upon thee. For I am the Lord thy God, the Holy One of Israel, thy Saviour" (Isa. 43:1-3).

The presence of the Lord is our great comfort. With Jesus hidden in God. He invites us: "Abide in me, and I in you." Be strong against a world full of unbelief, without being ashamed for your King. We must be spirit-filled soldiers and must fight to gain the victory, until Jesus comes. He is our strength now, and also in the last battle.

"In all these things we win an overwhelming victory through him who has proved his love for us" (Rom. 8:37, Phillips).

Hallelujah!
  Jesus was Victor!
    Jesus is Victor!
      Jesus will be Victor!

"He humbled himself by living a life of utter obedience, even to the extent of dying, and the death he died was the death of a common criminal. That is why God has now lifted him so high, and has given him the name beyond all names, so that at the name of Jesus 'every knee shall bow', whether in heaven or earth or under the earth. And that is why, in the end, 'Every tongue shall confess' that Jesus Christ is the Lord, to the glory of God the Father" (Phil. 2:8–11, Phillips).

That is why we stand with Jesus through the Holy Spirit on Victory ground. When *you* kneel before Him, will He be your Judge or your Saviour?

"For God, who commanded the light to shine out of darkness, hath shined in our hearts, to give the light of the knowledge of the glory of God in the face of Jesus Christ" (2 Cor. 4:6).